# The Woman's Day Book of HOUSE PLANTS

BY

*Jean Hersey*

ILLUSTRATED BY

*Harry Marinsky*

INTRODUCTION BY

*Dr. Richard A. Howard*

DIRECTOR, ARNOLD ARBORETUM,
HARVARD UNIVERSITY

SIMON AND SCHUSTER
NEW YORK

The Editors of Woman's Day and Jean Hersey wish to thank Dr. Richard Alden Howard, Director of the Arnold Arboretum and Professor of Botany at Harvard University, for graciously making himself available for consultation on matters of a technical horticultural nature.

16   17   18   19   20   21   22   23   24   25

# Contents

Introduction by Dr. Richard A. Howard      7

The Joys of Window Gardening      9

Care and Upkeep      12

Twelve Ways to Be a Better Window Gardener      19

Kitchen Horticulture and Other Surprises      21

A Dictionary of House Plants      25

Seven Window Gardens      108

Index      123

# Introduction

Our pioneer forefathers planted gardens primarily for food, with a few plants for spices, sachets and dried bouquets. Today most of us have neither space nor need for farming, but the residual, perhaps inherited, urge to grow living plants still prevails. Instead of acres of crops and straight rows, we now focus on individual plants grown solely for our delight.

In the old American farmhouse only the most hardy of pot plants such as sansevieria and agapanthus could stand the indoor environment of fireplace heat, drafty noninsulated windows and limited illumination. Today your home offers a variety of environmental conditions suitable for many types of plants, and such devices as humidifiers, fluorescent lighting and heating cables can be used to modify a room or a corner for horticultural purposes.

Similarly the assortment of plants currently available for enjoyment has never been so great. The newest hybrids of horticulture and the most recent discoveries of the plant explorer are yours at reasonable prices.

Today the world is your garden. Within your walls you can grow plants from every continent on this earth. To help your indoor garden flourish is the aim of this accurate and comprehensive handbook.

RICHARD A. HOWARD
Director, The Arnold Arboretum
Harvard University

# The Joys of Window Gardening

Something rather wonderful occurs when the last flaming autumn leaves fall and turn brown, when November steals in with quiet tones, and snow flurries dance through gray days. The indoor garden comes into its own. In summer, a long border of delphiniums, a riot of zinnias, a neat row of vegetables, each has its particular delight. But in the fall nature rests, and the window gardener can concentrate on individual plants. In the small area of a windowsill every single plant comes into sharp focus. Whether you have one pot or sixteen, whether your indoor garden is in a country house, a business office or an apartment, each new shoot has a vital importance.

One potted plant is a garden—small scale. A single plant in its container becomes in itself a whole world. Water it, tend it, appreciate it. Watch it grow. Observe just how young leaves unfold and flower buds emerge in their season. Live with the plant through a year as it develops, burgeons, rests; the whole cycle of growth is intimately close. Becoming aware of each detail is a particular joy.

Some plants grow an inch a day; whenever you walk by you observe a change. The passion-vine tendrils are swinging loose for breakfast; by lunchtime they have discovered the string and twined. All day the prayer-plant leaves are at right angles to their stems; at dusk they angle upward like arms raised in thanksgiving.

You may have thought of aurora borealis as the phenomenon that occurs only in the August heavens on a clear, starry night when it is unusually cool. But aurora borealis is also a plant that occurs in your window garden, with sea-green leaves fading to pink and soft waxy pink flowers that last for months. Then there is the American wonder lemon, which grows fragrant flowers and huge green one-pound lemons at the same time. Do you know the seersucker plant with its nubby foliage? The plant that eats the flies in your kitchen is the venus flytrap. With nutmeg, apple, rose geraniums you raise your own sachets. The entire household will pause on a particular winter night for the annual flowering of the night-blooming cereus to watch the great one-foot flowers stirringly unfold to send their fragrance into every corner of the room.

When winter really takes over, we miss the smells of outdoors and the fragrances of growing things. How we welcome the scents in the window garden. A good number of flowers are chosen for the house because of their fragrance, and there are plants whose leaves, when gently crushed, perfume your fingers. In addition, after the morning foliage spray, that wonderful, warm, wet scent of growth itself blends all these individual fragrances together.

In the last few years commercial house-plant growers have taken great strides and come up with quantities of new material. They have developed, imported and propagated plants so that our windows may flourish with the exotic, the rare and unusual, as well as the beloved familiar plants. Even these have been improved in quality and sturdiness.

House plants today come in all colors and shapes, some with soft feathery foliage, some with stiff, shiny leaves or downy ones that are pleasant to feel. There are plants for sun, for shade, plants that thrive in living room, kitchen, family room or even bathroom. A number bloom in the fall, others in the spring, and a few send up flowers practically the year around. There are foliage plants whose colors are brilliant and gay, and others for creating a garden of cool, soft, varied shades of green.

Venture into new realms. Try varieties you have never grown before, never even known before. Choose colors that especially appeal. Select plants to fit not only your location as to sun and shade, but your decorative scheme, contemporary or traditional. Also choose plants that fit your living habits. If you are home only in the evening choose some flowers that are white, for they will stand out in the dim night light. Also grow some night-blooming plants. Among these pages are a wealth of all sorts from which to select.

It is easy to feel a genuine warmth and affection for these plants which become a vital part of your days. Each new fern frond that unrolls appears as a small miracle. And how natural to love the rose geranium that you can so readily share with friends. Buy one plant now and enjoy its spicy scent all winter in the house. Summer it on a sunny windowsill or in a sunny garden area. At the end of August cut it entirely apart and into six-inch pieces. Repot the pieces separately, being sure to set each cutting right side up. By December you will have perhaps two dozen or more plants that make superb—and thrifty—Christmas presents.

When you give your care, interest and affection to a garden of indoor plants they reward you with vibrant health, gay colors, assorted textures and myriad fragrances. House plants bring beauty and vitality to the spot where they live and they also weave a few strands of pure summer through the tapestry of short winter days.

Perhaps a window garden is at its best on a chilly winter day when icicles fringe the eaves, when the wind howls in the chimney, and when the sun shines in on your small indoor tropic. Friends come to visit, and the greenery, fragrance and flowers transform your room and enhance the occasion. Or perhaps you are alone, and this too is a high moment. You draw up a chair beside your plants, perhaps you water, spray foliage, turn a plant, trim off a straggle, or maybe you just sit. Soon your awareness quickens, you begin noticing new things. Here is a brand-new leaflet, here is a bud barely visible that wasn't there yesterday—a fragrance sweet and pungent envelops you.

Instinctively you reach out to touch the plants and feel the featheriness of the rabbit's-foot fern fronds, the firmness of the fan iris, the vitality of the sweet olive. When you tear yourself away from this moment and return to the world of household tasks, you are refreshed, and you bring to your day an added energy, an added joy.

# Care and Upkeep

The care of a window garden is brief and simple. What is involved first of all is the choice of a location, proper watering, feeding, and protection from insects. Next comes the matter of repotting, summer care, and what to do when a plant seems to be ailing. Lastly there is the great joy and satisfaction derived from making slips and cuttings to enlarge your own collection or to share with fellow window gardeners.

## LOCATION—WHERE?

Almost every room in the house presents a possible location for a window garden. Living room, bedroom (if there is not too great a drop in temperature at night), kitchen and even bath may all be good choices. What is the best exposure? North, south, east and west are all fine. The important aspect of location is to select the proper plant for the proper place. There are countless varieties for the sunny window, many others prefer shade, and some adapt to both. With the right plant in the right spot you are off to an ideal start. The preferred location is given for each plant described in this book.

If you have a table before the window, a wide sill, or a radiator you can turn off and whose top you can use, have a galvanized tray made (at the hardware store) to fit the space. Equally good and easier to come by would be a nice clear plastic tray, available in housewares or variety stores. Fill the tray with natural colored pebbles and water. The pebbles conveniently raise the pots above the water (this is not necessary for a few varieties, including the umbrella sedge, which thrive with wet feet). The tray of constantly evaporating water adds moisture to the surrounding air. It also facilitates the needed daily lukewarm water foliage spray, and incidentally helps avoid drenching the floor.

## WATERING

How do you water house plants enough and not too much? A good general rule, unless otherwise indicated with specific plants, is to soak each one thoroughly with room-temperature water, and then let the earth pretty well dry out before soaking again. This is what is meant by "average watering" in this book. For their health and well-being, most plant roots need air at times as well as water. When the soil is dry, air can permeate the earth particles.

A mist spray on the foliage is welcome to most plants, especially ivies, ferns, orchids and philodendrons. But hairy-leaved varieties such as African violets, geraniums, gloxinias, and *Siderasis fuscata* do *not* benefit from having their leaves wet. Instead of using water from the tap, if you can collect rain water or melted snow and warm it to room temperature and use this, you will do your plants a great favor. City water is often filled with chemicals that do the plants no great harm perhaps, but no great good either. All are better off with natural, untreated water.

## PLANT FOOD

Almost every house plant does best with a weekly fertilizer (except right after flowering, which is usually a rest period). While each watering frees food elements in the soil and renders them available to foraging roots, a potted plant is not like one loose in the earth with unlimited soil available to provide sustenance. All too soon the pot rim is reached by a searching rootlet. Therefore, a little extra nourishment is of value. A great assortment of plant-food tablets, powders and liquids are on the market. Fish-emulsion fertilizer, with its distinctive smell, but at the same time great powers of energizing and stirring plant growth, is one of the best. Certain varieties of house-plant foods you dilute before using and water on the soil. Some of the tablets you simply tuck into the earth, and each subsequent watering releases more of the desired nourishing ingredients.

## THE UNINVITED PEST

As a healthy, well-adjusted person seldom gets sick, so, theoretically, a healthy plant set in a proper location and given good care seldom succumbs to insects, blights or other ailments. Occasionally, however, despite our best efforts, and often for no apparent reason, some favorite develops a problem or an invasion of insects descends unexpectedly.

*Aphids* are the tiny gray or black creatures that attach themselves thickly to the new tips of ivy or other plants. They are partial always to fresh young growth, which without doubt is the tenderest. Aphids are the little "cows" of the ants, who come and milk them of the life juices they have sucked from the foliage of your plant. Of course the plant thus milked soon languishes. A clear water spray agitates the aphids and often frees the plant of them.

*Mealy bugs* are the white cotton-like pests that nestle in the branches or at the leaf joints of a number of plants. They are to be found particularly under foliage where the daily water spray doesn't reach. Clear water dispenses with mealy bugs quite promptly. But it is often difficult to locate and soak all of them, and they multiply with great rapidity.

When mealy bugs first appear, and if there aren't too many, a firm hosing with the spray from the kitchen sink eliminates them. (To prevent the dirt from splashing out of the pot during this process tuck foil tightly around the plant stem, and fold it over the pot rim before you start.) Another way to get rid of these white cottony pests is to touch each cluster with a small paintbrush dipped in alcohol and spray afterwards with clear water.

*Red spiders* the size of a speck of soot may infest some of the leaves. Look for these on the undersides of the ivy foliage. A thorough soaking also disposes of these.

*White flies,* small as a speck, will sometimes be found congregating on the undersides of the leaves. Nicotiana, fuchsia and lantana are particularly susceptible. Dip in a soapy solution of nicotine insecticide—directions are given on the product—every few days until the plant is free of them.

*Scale*—small flat, or rounded scalelike insects—often appears as bits of miniature "armor" lying flat on the foliage of the ivies, sea onion and some others. A soft brush or wet sponge and soapy water removes them.

If the simpler controls don't free your plants of these insect pests, a nicotine insecticide is extremely effective. This is one of the best because its poison doesn't built up in the soil or linger in the air but soon disperses. Rotenone and pyrethrum are other safe sprays for the window gardens in a household with children and pets.

Here is an easy way to use insecticides on small and medium-sized plants. Take a large pan or bucket. Into this measure out a solution of insecticide and water, following directions on the package with great care and accuracy. Add soap flakes—never detergent—to form a light sudsy consistency. Cover the pot soil with newspaper or foil to keep the earth in place. Holding the plant on its side or upside down, dip it several times in the solution. Let it stand a few minutes and dip again.

If you have pebble trays of water beneath the pots to protect the floor, you can spray a troubled plant where it stands. Small house-plant sprays are available which spread their mist over only a limited area. However, since healthy plants are best unsprayed, it is usually a good idea to remove the infected one and treat it separately in the kitchen or shower. Actually it is wise to keep a sick plant apart, as diseases and insects tend to spread.

SOMETHING BETTER THAN POISONS

There is another way of freeing your house plants from insects and at the same time introducing a new and delightful pet into the family. Buy a chameleon and let him loose in the window garden. This interesting little creature will dine on aphids and mealy bugs, red spiders, and even a housefly or two if one comes within range. Buy a pair and you will not only be free of pests but in late winter will enjoy watching their courting. The gentleman turns bright green when in love. So, in a hue of brilliant emerald he trails after his lady up and down the stems of the vines. All the while he blows out a small orange bubble at his throat. The lady, ever a little ahead, glances back invitingly over her shoulder to be sure her spouse is following. Your pair may even have young. And newly hatched chameleon infants are enchanting.

## REPOTTING

The procedure of repotting house plants is an important part of their care and upkeep. Annually in spring or fall most all of them will need new earth to grow in, or at least some fresh soil replacing the top inch or two of soil in the pot. Many will also require a larger-sized container. At various other times of year certain plants can also be repotted. A good rule is to repot after the blooms fade, as at that time the plant usually enters into a rest period. If, incidentally, you don't want a plant to grow any larger when you repot, prune both roots and top using a sharp knife or pruners.

Window-garden soil must *feel* right. Take a handful of earth and hold it in your hand. Squeeze it; it should hold its shape until touched, and should then crumble. If it has too much sand in it, it will not hold its shape when squeezed. If it contains too much clay, it will not crumble. The soil must also smell right—never sour or strong. Good-smelling soil, when slightly moist, possesses a fresh, vibrant, growing scent, rather like the earth after a May shower when the sun comes out.

Certain plants like special kinds of soil. This is noted in the caption accompanying each plant. But a good average blend for most consists of a mixture of two parts of fresh top soil, one of coarse building sand, one of compost or leaf mold or well-rotted cow manure. A few pieces of charcoal in the pot helps to keep it sweet. Mix all this up and strain through a quarter- or half-inch wire mesh before using.

This is the ideal soil to use. But, of course, anything approaching it will probably do very well. Apartment dwellers are always able to buy good potting soil by the bagful from the florist or variety store. House plants are more adaptable than people realize. While it is always good to aim for the ideal, it is surprising and comforting how often they will adjust to something far less.

Everyone has his own system of repotting plants. There is really no one and only way of doing this. Our procedure is as follows—and I don't say it's any better than yours. If using clay pots, soak them to start lest in the first few days they absorb the water intended for newly established roots. Plastic or glazed containers are equally good for indoor gardening. They hold the moisture longer and therefore are excellent in a hot, dry room or a steam-heated apartment. Sometimes these pots hold the moisture too long and the soil becomes soggy. Be sure they have a good drainage hole. Plants in glazed, plastic, or china containers need less water than those in clay pots.

When repotting, place a piece of broken crock or a flat stone over the bottom hole so the soil doesn't wash out. Then add a one-inch layer of finely broken crock at the bottom of the pot to insure good drainage. The plant center or crown should rest on a little cushion of soil and be nearly an inch below the pot rim and just covered with earth. With a pencil or similar stick, or your fingers, firm the dirt among the roots. Fill the pot, leaving enough space at the top for watering—about a half to one inch. Sometimes in repotting an old plant the roots need not be disturbed at all. When shifting to a larger-sized container, merely pack fresh new earth in the space around the pot rim.

If a plant appears weak and ailing and you don't quite know what is wrong, you can often revive it with repotting. When you take it out of the container, examine it carefully. You may discover that some of the roots are rotted and need to be trimmed off, or that the soil has become moldy, perhaps from too much watering. You may even find insects or diseases at the roots which were quite invisible from the surface. With the diseased part trimmed away, fresh, live soil to grow in, and the plant top pruned back, it has a good chance to revive.

## SUMMERING IN THE GARDEN

Most indoor plants benefit from a summer outdoors. When you live in the country this is usually possible and easy. Choose a place where the soil is sandy, where drainage is excellent, and where there is no drip from overhead eaves. Let this area be one of partial shade. Even if they thrive in full sun indoors in winter, most varieties of house plants find the change from glass-filtered sun to direct outdoor sun too great.

In the garden, sink each pot to its rim in the earth. Almost all plants do better to remain in their pots. When they grow loose in the soil for several months they are apt to find the adjustment back to a pot difficult.

House plants summering in the garden need to be watered only during dry spells. With average rainfall you can almost forget them during their outdoor sojourn and they will flourish in a heartening manner. In September, or at least two weeks before you turn on the furnace, move the indoor garden back to the windowsill. It is important that they all have a week or two in the house before the central heating goes on. When you remove the pots from the soil, scrub the dirt off the outside. This is another opportunity for repotting those plants that need it.

## FOR APARTMENT DWELLERS

While a garden is the ideal place to summer your house plants if you live in the country, apartment dwellers successfully move them to a shady window, and they will do just about as well. Where it is suggested that individual plants be summered outdoors, those of you who have no gardens may interpret this to mean a shady window—one that is open a good bit of the time during the warm months. Apartment dwellers also may leave them in the same window and protect them, if necessary, from the hot summer sun. And of course they don't want to be placed in the direct draft of an air-conditioner.

## Indoor Plant Nursery

All window gardeners need a small nursery for cuttings. Friends may present you with slips of their plants, and you'll want to multiply your own favorites. Any abandoned aquarium or glass container with a glass top, such as an apothecary jar, will make a fine nursery. Spread a layer of sand, compost or vermiculite two to three inches deep on the bottom and put your cuttings in this. Keep it moist but never wet and soggy. Broken charcoal from the fireplace stirred in prevents it from souring. Lift the top once a day for a few moments of air. This container is best kept where there is good light but *no sun*. Sun causes the rooting medium to develop mold. Practically any kind of cutting from your favorite ivy to your most unusual begonia will sprout in a few weeks in such a nursery. If the nursery happens to be large enough, a sick plant will often revive if set for a couple of weeks in this humid atmosphere.

## Sixteen Useful Aids for the Window Gardener

1. A rubber syringe that releases a fine spray.
2. A long-spouted watering can.
3. Pots of various sizes.
4. Charcoal (from the fireplace if you have one).
5. Plant food.
6. A sharp knife or pruning shears for root or top pruning.
7. A small trowel.
8. A pencil or similar stick for firming soil when you repot.
9. A kitchen fork or apple corer for occasionally loosening and stirring the surface earth in flowerpots.
10. A selection of potting soils, including average garden soil, sand and compost.
11. A soft brush for dusting leaves of African violets and other plushy foliage plants.
12. A stiff scrub brush for cleaning clay pots.
13. A bottle of nicotine spray for mealy bugs, aphids, etc.
14. A small-sized spray for insecticides.
15. A bridge lamp or gooseneck lamp, and a 100-watt bulb.
16. A fluorescent lamp to light that difficult dim corner where you want to grow something.

# Twelve Ways to
# Be a Better Window Gardener

To keep a window garden thriving there are certain definite rules to follow, certain musts. There are, in addition, a number of favors you can do your plants. While not absolutely necessary to their survival, these extras cause your plants to flourish and become increasingly healthy and beautiful.

The longer you garden in the house the more you learn about the subject, and so often by trial and error. Also, the more of your own particular tricks and methods you evolve and practice, the better the results, and the greater the satisfactions.

Here are a dozen of our tricks:

1. On chilly nights slip a sheet of plastic between the window glass and the plants lest some leaves touch the icy panes and become frostbitten.
2. Trim off dead or wilted leaves from each plant and burn these, as they often harbor diseases or insects.
3. Prune to keep every plant shapely.
4. Turn pots frequently so plants do not develop a permanent window-ward list.
5. Set plants far enough apart so the adjoining leaves don't tangle together. All plants prefer elbow room. With a little space around them their full shape can also be better appreciated.
6. Plants like fresh air. At least once a day open a window or door, not directly on your house plants, if weather is cold, but nearby.
7. A 100-watt bulb in a lamp two feet from the foliage and turned on from dusk until 10 P.M. each night costs but a few cents and extends valuable light hours on short winter days.
8. Glass shelves across the pane partway up extend the growing area and make a fine place for trailing ivies and vines.
9. Loosen the earth in the plant containers every two or three weeks with an old apple corer or kitchen fork.
10. Use a little rooting powder to multiply some of your favorite begonias, philodendrons and ivies. Cut four-inch stems, dip the bottom end into the white powder. Set to root in pots of vermicu-

lite or sandy soil. Keep slightly moist and out of the direct sunlight until new growth starts.

11. A pot whose soil is dry is lighter to lift than one you have just watered. You come to learn, just by lifting the container, whether it needs more water or not. A plant growing and flowering takes more water than one that has finished its blooming period or one that has not yet come into flower. This subtle knowing that all window gardeners acquire is half the fun and satisfaction.

12. Don't hesitate to throw away plants which have had their day. This latter is sometimes difficult because of sentiment or, should I say, sentimentality. It is kinder to make a new cutting from an old favorite given you by a beloved friend. Let the old plant meet a peaceful demise, preferably in the compost where it will eventually contribute valuable growing elements to something else. The thriving new young plant will be a much better reminder of your friend than that old overgrown unwieldy one.

# Kitchen Horticulture and Other Surprises

Direct from the kitchen comes special enchantment for the window garden with particular appeal for the children and grandchildren in your life.

The friendly and familiar carrot that is supposed to make your hair curl and help you see in the dark contributes a bright spot of color at the window. Growing foliage of beets, parsnips, turnips and carrots makes delightful table centerpieces. A lone sweet potato will luxuriate as it grows. Pineapple tops, citrus seeds and herbs all make attractive and unusual plants.

CARROT "FERN"    Make carrot into a fern in the following manner: Scoop out the inside of a large firm carrot, fill the hollow with water and keep it filled. Then run a piece of wire through the top and hang the carrot in the window with partial sun. In a week or two feathery fern-like foliage emerges up and down the sides, greenery that grows until it all but conceals the fat, orange carrot shape.

BEETS   CARROTS   PARSNIPS   TURNIPS    Cut three-quarters of an inch from the top of the vegetable, leaving any existing foliage, and set the cutting upright in a flat bowl in a half inch of water. It will begin to sprout in about a week and will last for perhaps a month. A combination of any or all of these makes a delightful table centerpiece. Beet leaves are reddish, oval and smooth. Those of the carrot are bright green and feathery. Tiny new leaves of parsnips and turnips have a different form and texture and blend well with carrots and beets.

SWEET POTATO    Grows into a trailing vine. Stick toothpicks in the sides and suspend potato half above water in a tall glass. Set in a light, but not sunny, window until it begins to grow. Don't be disappointed if nothing happens for several weeks. It's slow to start. Change water occasionally. The vine itself as it emerges from the potato enjoys sun, but the glass of water should be shaded.

LENTILS

Place a handful in a shallow bowl of water and watch them develop in about a week into a cluster of delicate greenery.

AVOCADO

It isn't necessary to start an avocado with tooth-picks in water. Plant one, pointed end up, just under the soil in a pot of good garden loam. Water regularly. Within a few weeks a small stem should appear and begin to grow.

PINEAPPLE

Slice off the top of a fresh pineapple and plant it one inch deep in a pot of earth. The saw-edged leaves soon expand into an attractive blue-green rosette that lasts all winter.

GRAPEFRUIT
ORANGE

Soak seeds for two or three days in water. Then plant them a half inch deep and one inch apart in a low container of soil. They will sprout into seedlings with rich, dark-green, glossy foliage. Within a few weeks you have a charming six-inch forest.

LETTUCE SEEDS
KENTUCKY BLUE-
GRASS SEED

Plant them on a sponge set in a saucer of water.

GRASS SEED

Try these on an old dried corncob held upright with stones in a flat dish of water.
Sow leftovers from the lawn on an ordinary brick resting half submerged in a bowl of water.
Note: All varieties of seed create soft and appealing bright-green notes for the indoor garden. And plain green grass growing indoors in January is fascinating. If not trimmed it turns into a wind-blown tangle as interesting and decorative as many

a fern. You can also shear it with scissors and have a small pot of "lawn."

CHIVES

A chive plant in the window garden contributes flavor to soups, salads and scrambled eggs. Toward spring it unfolds furry lavender flowers.

BASIL

In Italy there is an old legend that a woman who wants to be understood should wear a sprig of basil in her hair, and in England long ago a host, to brighten and cheer his guests, would serve them basil. A little six-inch basil plant thrives in a sunny window garden, and the leaves may be dropped in soup or salad to the improvement of both—and who knows, perhaps to the benefit of the family's disposition as well.

EGGSHELLS

Get a head start on Easter in midwinter! Dye some eggs in all the cheerful spring colors and crack each one evenly into two parts. Fill each half-shell with garden soil and plant with a pinch of alyssum or petunia seeds. The gay tinted "pots" will stand upright in a small tray or flat bowl of sand. These will flower for Easter, and for several weeks thereafter. The little eggshells may also be suspended in string cradles. If you think you would like to make a mobile, here are the ingredients of an irresistible one.

*Dictionary*
*of House Plants*

# A Dictionary of House Plants

One hundred and ninety-one plants are pictured and described in the following pages. Some old favorites, like geraniums and begonias, have been cultivated as house plants for hundreds of years. Others have only recently been developed for your window garden by the commercial plant grower. Whichever ones you select, never hesitate to follow your own hunch or intuition in caring for your plants.

In the directions for growing each plant, ideal conditions are suggested. Many will thrive in and adapt themselves to less than ideal surroundings. You may discover that a variety recommended for a sunny window is doing very well in part shade. There is plenty of territory that has not been covered in window gardening and ample room for the untried. When something is wrong with a plant, let this be an indication to exercise your imagination and ingenuity. Try different soil and location, and vary the watering and other procedures.

In each description, an estimate of the size of the plant is given. However, plants grow differently in different parts of the country. An indoor geranium in California or Florida may grow to six feet, while the same variety in a New England window may pause at fifteen inches. Consider the height given, therefore, as only approximate.

In making cuttings, where a stalk six inches long is suggested, a four-inch, two-inch or even an eight-inch one will often do just as well. Follow only the directions that seem right and expedient to you, and always consider your particular location and climate. Frequently I have suggested pruning foliage for compactness. If you like casual, sprawling plants, by all means let them remain so. There is no law that they must be compact. It is purely a matter of preference. Again, the temperature mentioned in the caption is the preferred one, but not necessarily the one and only. Many varieties will adapt to other degrees of heat or coolness.

## AFRICAN VIOLET (*Saintpaulia ionantha*)

A plant of temperament, character, and beauty. Flowers prolifically even in a north window, as long as there is fine light. Thrives in bathroom or kitchen, loves warm nights and steamy air. Blue, white, pink, lavender, purple, double, single, charming flowers. If your plants are flourishing keep right on with whatever you are doing for them. If not, or if you would like larger and more abundant blooms, try the following: Water with lukewarm water and from the saucer beneath. Keep temperature day and night 70° F. or slightly higher. Let soil dry thoroughly between waterings. If you are using wick-fed pots, let wick become dry as a bone before again filling bottom container with water.

LOCATION: North, east, west window, kitchen, bathroom. Filtered sunshine or none, but excellent light is vital.

HEIGHT: Up to 6 inches.

SOIL: Rich, light soil with some sand and leaf mold or compost in each pot, or use African Violet commercial soil mix. Feed regularly with African Violet fertilizer.

WATERING: See above.

PROPAGATION: Separate extra crowns with sharp knife, leaving roots attached to each. New plants may flower in a month or less. Or cut a leaf with one-inch stem, set in vermiculite, sand, soil or plain water. Several new plantlets develop from each leaf and bloom one year later.

27

◀ ALOE, CANDELABRA (*Aloe arborescens*)

A thorny treelike succulent with graceful upreaching branches. It grows well in steam-heated modern rooms. Easily propagated.

LOCATION: Thrives in full sun. Will tolerate partial sun.

HEIGHT: To 15 inches, when pot-grown. In tropical gardens, sometimes to 15 feet.

SOIL: Gritty, sandy soil or ordinary garden earth with sand added. Must not be too rich. Perfect drainage needed.

WATERING: Soil should be kept rather dry.

PROPAGATION: New four- to eight-inch plantlets can be cut or broken from the base of the main stem. The bottom ends should be planted two to four inches deep in soil.

AMAZON LILY (*Eucharis grandiflora*) ▶

Each pure-white blossom unfurls to reveal a pale trumpet-like green cup filled with feathery white stamens. Blooms in January and February. Grows wild by the acre all through Central America.

LOCATION: Partial shade in a warm room.

HEIGHT: Medium—up to 15 inches.

SOIL: Rich, with compost or humus added. Grow plant in a good-sized container with plenty of root room.

WATERING: Never let plant completely dry out until flowers pass. Then keep soil rather dry for several weeks while it rests.

FRAGRANCE: Subtle scent suggests fresh sweet lemons.

ANTHURIUM (*Anthurium andraeanum*)

Exotic waxy "flowers" of pink, red, white, orange, salmon, or coral; last literally months on the plant. What appears to be a flower is really a bract, or form of leaf. The curving tongue or spadix, in the center of the bract, is actually a cluster of tiny flowers. Give plant food every couple of weeks.

LOCATION: Warm, humid atmosphere. Filtered sun.

HEIGHT: Tall—up to 2 feet.

SOIL: Rich loamy mixture with sphagnum moss, charcoal, sand, leaf mold added.

WATERING: More than average. Never let the soil completely dry out. Spray foliage daily.

PROPAGATION: By division. Roots readily separate in the spring to form new plants.

SPECIAL CARE: Cover with sphagnum moss and keep moist any roots that tend to heave out of the pot soil. Keep leaves clean by washing often with soapy water.

▼

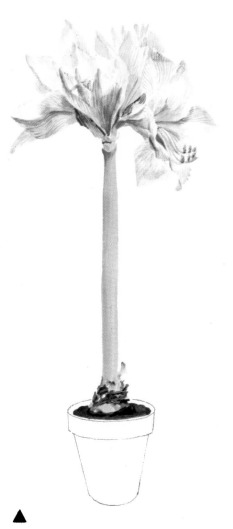

▲

AMARYLLIS (*Hippeastrum* species)

These stirring blossoms are so large they scarcely look real. Buy bulbs in the fall. Set each in a container *only one inch wider than the bulb,* with the top half of the bulb above the earth. Let it grow in a cool shady corner for four weeks while roots develop. Then give it sun and fertilizer. Blooms in eight to twelve weeks. Flowers may be salmon, pink, red, or white. Blooms year after year and does especially well when summered in the garden; the pot should be sunk up to the rim in a semi-shaded, windless spot. It may also be summered in an east or west window.

LOCATION: Sun.

HEIGHT: Tall—to 2½ feet.

SOIL: Good rich garden loam.

WATERING: Soak thoroughly, let dry, and then water again.

ANTHURIUM (*Anthurium crystallinum*)

A dramatic foliage plant of large heart-shaped green leaves soft and velvety to touch. Each one sparkles with silvery crystallized veins. The stems are reddish, and the main stalk almost furry. Foliage varies in pattern and color.

LOCATION: Adapts to any exposure.

HEIGHT: Medium—to 15 inches.

SOIL: Rich loamy earth mixed with leaf mold, charcoal, and sphagnum moss.

WATERING: Average. Soil should be allowed to dry between thorough waterings.

PROPAGATION: By division of roots at repotting time.

SPECIAL CARE: Foliage should be kept clean by frequent washings.

ANTHURIUM (*Anthurium* ▶ *scherzerianum*)

Like *Anthurium andraeanum*, this tropical beauty has exotic "flowers" and handsome foliage. Colorful heart-shaped bracts resemble wind-filled boat sails. The bracts may be white, pink, or red, and they are often spotted. They last for months and one follows another almost the year round.

HEIGHT: Tall—to 2 feet.

LOCATION and other requirements are the same as for *Anthurium andraeanum*.

ARTILLERY PLANT (*Pilea microphylla*)

Fresh from tropical America comes this delightful window-garden plant. The foliage is light green and succulent, somewhat fernlike. Small clusters of blossoms grow at leaf axils. When touched, these flowers respond by puffing out small whiffs of pollen "dust."

LOCATION: East or west window ideal. Prefers partial sun but must have strong light.

HEIGHT: Medium—to 15 inches.

SOIL: Ordinary garden earth.

WATERING: Soil should be kept moist but never soggy.

PROPAGATION: Cuttings root readily.

▲

## ASPARAGUS FERN, EMERALD FEATHER (*Asparagus sprengeri*)

The tumbling sprays of emerald green have a feathery fernlike quality, but the plant thrives with less humidity than a true fern. Trim to keep the size and shape desired. Small, fragrant pink blooms subsequently ripen into coral-red berries. To be sure of berries you need plants of both sexes.

LOCATION: Filtered sunlight, east or west window.

HEIGHT: Low; trails and spreads. An excellent basket plant.

SOILS Average garden loam.

WATERING: Soak, permit to dry, and again water thoroughly.

PROPAGATION: By division of roots. Or pot berries, an inch beneath the soil.

## AURORA BOREALIS PLANT (*Kalanchoe fedtschenkoi marginata*) ▶

Perfect for apartments where the air is warm and lacks humidity. When grown in full sun the margins of the blue-green leaves turn pink; in partial shade they remain white. Deep coral-pink flowers last from January to spring. Summer in a semishady garden spot or windowsill.

LOCATION: Full sun for bloom.

HEIGHT: To 15 inches.

SOIL: Gritty sandy earth, not too rich, but with good drainage.

WATERING: Let soil remain dry three or four days, then water sparingly. Water more if the leaves become limp, less if they yellow and drop.

PROPAGATION: In the fall, plant four- or eight-inch cuttings in two or three inches of soil. Do not overwater the cuttings at first lest they rot. Water lightly once or perhaps twice a week.

31

◀ AUSTRALIAN FLAME PEA
(*Chorizema cordatum*)

Sometimes called flowering oak. A rare but easy indoor "sweet pea" whose orange, yellow, or purple blooms are abundantly produced in late winter or spring. Summer this plant: Sink pot in the earth in a shady part of the garden, or place it in a north window.

LOCATION: East or west window.

HEIGHT: Climbs and trails, or may be kept to any size or shape desired by pruning.

SOIL: Ordinary garden loam.

WATERING: Soak, let dry, and water again. Soil should be drier while plant rests during the summer.

PROPAGATION: Root cuttings made in the spring in soil or sand, setting the bottom end two or three inches under the surface.

AZTEC LILY (*Stapelia gigantea*) ▶

A member of the milkweed family. From a tangle of soft flexible spines emerge a number of small green balloons. Daily these increase in size, becoming of geometric shape and design. One morning, and petal by petal, the largest will be the first to unfold into a strange star-shaped blossom, brown-patterned, decorated with crossbars.

LOCATION: Full sun. Thrives in hot dry atmosphere.

HEIGHT: 4 to 6 inches, also trails down over the pot rim.

SOIL: Gritty sandy earth. Good drainage vital.

WATERING: Perhaps once or twice a week. Soil should be kept fairly dry most of the time. When the plant needs more water, the spiny stems go limp.

PROPAGATION: Any branch may be broken off, and about 2 inches of the stem end planted in a separate container. Within a year the new plant will flower.

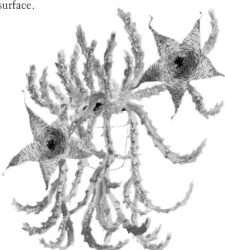

BABY TEARS (*Helxine soleirolii*)

Spreads its greenery over the fields of Corsica. Also flourishes in Ireland and is often called Irish moss. Straying twiggy branches are all but hidden beneath the tiny bright-green leaves of dewdrop size. Sheds foliage annually, leaving the plant a welter of wiry stems, but new leaves soon appear.

LOCATION: Filtered sun. East or west window, or even north.

◀ HEIGHT: Low and spreading.

SOIL: Average garden loam.

WATERING: More than average except when resting.

PROPAGATION: Very easy. A little cluster of the brown twigs may be pressed into a container of soil and kept watered. For a charming effect, the twigs may be planted around the edges of three soil-filled pots of graduated sizes, placed one on top of the other for a tiered effect.

AZALEA (*Rhododendron* 'Albert Elizabeth')

Pink, red, or white, single or double flowers appear in the late winter, and plant continues to bloom for many weeks if kept in a sunny window and in a *cool* room. Summer in the garden in a sheltered semishady spot. Repot annually with fresh soil. Trim the plant—both roots and tops—lest it grow leggy and sparse. Feed weekly during the fall and winter with acid fertilizer.

LOCATION: Partial sun. East or west exposure.

HEIGHT: Small to medium.

SOIL: Rich earth with leaf mold and peat moss added. Prefers acidity such as rhododendrons and camellias need.

WATERING: Likes high humidity. Never let the soil dry thoroughly.

## GENERAL CARE OF BEGONIAS

LOCATION: East or west window, partial sun filtered through a curtain or other plants.

HEIGHT: Begonias have a habit of sprawling and becoming leggy. Prune drastically to keep full and bushy. Turn the pot occasionally to maintain symmetrical growth.

SOIL: Rich garden loam with leaf mold added. Perfect drainage is vital.

WATERING: More than average. But if leaves drop, you are overwatering.

PROPAGATION: Four- to six-inch cuttings pruned from the plant and set one or two inches deep in vermiculite, soil or sand will rapidly grow into new plants. Or lay a leaf or two on the surface of a pot filled with soil and cover over with plastic. Poke a few holes in the plastic for ventilation. New plantlets form at leaf edge.

SPECIAL CARE: If possible, summer begonias in the garden, setting them out after all danger of frost is past. Bury the container up to the rim in a partly shaded windless place. Repot in the fall with fresh earth.

BEGONIA (*Begonia haageana*)

Sometimes called *Begonia scharfii*. Most attractive bronze-green scalloped downy leaves with red undersides and pink veining decorate this plant. Shell-pink bearded flowers, hanging in clusters among the foliage, blossom at almost every season of the year.

▼

33

BEGONIA 'Corallina de Lucerna' ▶
A vigorous angel-wing type. The large
dark spotty leaves are scarlet beneath.
Clusters of showy pendent crimson flowers
appear almost continually the year round.

◀ BEGONIA 'Dancing Girl'
A casual windblown plant with undulating leaves curling under at the tips.
The foliage is scarlet, silvery pink and
green all at once. Red flowers, unfolding
in small clusters, appear almost continually.

BEGONIA, EYELASH (*Begonia boweri*) ▶
Small ruffled leaves and no two alike.
Each one, a work of art in itself, is down-
covered and has an "eyelash" of dark
markings around the rim. The leaf stems
are orange-scarlet. In winter clusters of
small white blossoms tinged with pink
appear on graceful arching stems.

▲

BEGONIA 'Fern'

A spreading trailing plant of great appeal. Tiny jagged-edged leaves spread up and down sprays of arching red stems. Dainty white blossoms are sprinkled over the foliage.

BEGONIA 'Iron Cross'
The leaves, which are pebbled and jagged-edged, are often frilled and ruffled, and always downy. Each one bears the chocolate-colored pattern of a cross on the silver-green background.

▼

◄ BEGONIA 'Merry Christmas'
Each gay leaf has a maroon star in the center, surrounded by a rippling pink pattern, next a pattern of white, then green, and finally an edging of maroon. The plant grows compact and full with foliage that overlaps.

BEGONIA (*Begonia semperflorens* ► 'Fiesta')
A strong and lusty plant with waxy cup-shaped leaves. The foliage is sometimes bronze-red, sometimes green, and often both colors. Red flowers are borne in small rosette-like clusters. True to its name, this begonia seldom stops blooming.

## BIRD OF PARADISE (*Strelitzia reginae*)

An exotic tropical plant, a member of the banana family. Each blue-and-yellow flower emerges from a bright purple bract to form the shape of a bird's head complete with feathery and regal crest.

LOCATION: Good light. East window, partial sun.

HEIGHT: Tall—up to 3 feet. Grow with ample space.

SOIL: Average garden loam.

WATERING: Water lightly in the late fall. Begin in January to increase water supply. Feed weekly while "birds" form and come into bloom.

PROPAGATION: By division. Pot new shoots that develop at base of main stalk.

▼

▲

## BILLBERGIA (*Billbergia* 'Fantasia')

This bromeliad—a member of a large family of air plants related to the pine-apple—has long streaming leaves occasionally spotted creamy white. In brilliant sun the foliage turns bronze. Red and indigo flowers emerge from a crimson sheath.

LOCATION: Strong sun preferred, but must have good light.

HEIGHT: To 2 feet.

SOIL: Equal parts garden loam, sharp sand, and osmunda fiber. Put 2 inches of coarse drainage, broken crock, or pebbles at the bottom of the container. Set the base of the leaves above the soil.

WATERING: Plenty of water at the roots and a frequent foliage spray.

PROPAGATION: Pot the offshoots from the base of the plant when they have grown woody.

SPECIAL CARE: A Living Vase, it likes water in the "cups" formed where the leaves join the stem. If possible fill these with rain water at room temperature.

## BOUGAINVILLEA 'Barbara Karst'

This tropical climber may be pruned to pot size and it will unfold scarlet flower bracts that remain fresh and lovely for months. To keep plant perpetually in flower, trim stems back to the main stalk as soon as blossoms fade. Summer it in a shady part of the garden, if possible.

LOCATION: Grow in a cool place, ideally at 60° F., never higher than 70° F. Needs sun but will not thrive in a warm, dry atmosphere.

HEIGHT: Climbs and trails. Keep pruned to size and shape desired.

SOIL: Regular garden loam.

WATERING: Keep soil moderately wet most of the time.

## BLOODLEAF (*Iresine herbstii*)

Not only the foliage but even the fleshy branches of this easy-to-grow house plant are crimson! When the sun shines through them, the whole room catches the light. Set plant outdoors in summer, if possible. Prune to prevent legginess and repot annually with fresh soil.

LOCATION: Full sun. In partial sun the leaves become paler in color.

HEIGHT: Low; climbs and trails.

SOIL: Average garden earth.

WATERING: Let soil dry between soakings.

PROPAGATION: Snip a few fleshy stems and pot them in a separate container.

## BOUVARDIA (*Bouvardia Ternifolia* 'Fire Chief')

Named after the French doctor Bouvard, who not only loved gardening but used many of nature's herbs in his prescriptions. Clusters of vivid red waxy-textured flowers keep opening all winter from amidst the attractive greenery of this half-trailing plant. The plant literally blooms its life away in a single season. Never try to hold it over the summer.

LOCATION: Must be grown in a cool place. Preferred temperature 60° F. Full sun.

HEIGHT: Rangy and spreading. Grows to 1½ feet.

SOIL: Rich garden loam.

WATERING: Soak daily, and syringe the foliage with water at room temperature.

FRAGRANCE: Rich tropical scent. A white variety resembling our garden nicotiana is especially fragrant.

PROPAGATION: Plant cuttings of fresh green branch ends in the spring for next year's bloom.

**BOXWOOD** (*Buxus microphylla japonica*) ▶

A miniature small-leaved indoor shrub with compact dense foliage—attractive in a dish garden when small. Increase the interest and charm of your window garden by providing plants with various contrasting textures. Boxwood is a little bush that brings, in its smooth, firm, rich green foliage, a striking contrast to the soft feathery fern fronds, the downy begonia leaves, and the fleshy scarlet bloodleaf.

LOCATION: Full sun.

HEIGHT: Low. Keep shrub trimmed to maintain a compact and rounded shape.

SOIL: Average garden loam.

WATERING: Average.

◀ **BRAZILIAN EDELWEISS** (*Rechsteineria leucotricha*)

Leaves covered with silver down are soft as a kitten's ear. Pink tubular flowers appear in late winter. Summer plant in the garden, if possible, in an area of morning and afternoon sun where there is noon shade for a few hours. When new fall growth starts, trim off the old foliage, which tends to die back anyway, to ensure bloom.

LOCATION: Full sun. Warm room where temperature never drops lower than 60° F.

HEIGHT: Low, to 6 inches.

SOIL: Garden loam with humus added.

WATERING: Water moderately and let soil dry between waterings.

◀ **BRAZILIAN FIRECRACKER** (*Manettia bicolor*)

A South American import that is a prolific bloomer. Fabulous tubular yellow-tipped red blossoms like firecrackers emerge at every leaf axil. The plant itself tends to sprawl and straggle, so be a little tough from time to time, and trim it into shape. Keep plant indoors the year round; it cannot endure the winds and storms of an outdoor summer climate.

LOCATION: Full sun. South window in winter, east or west window in summer.

HEIGHT: Low; trails and spreads. Grows well in a hanging basket.

SOIL: Average garden loam.

WATERING: Keep soil moist but never soggy.

BROWALLIA (*Browallia speciosa major*) ▶

From tropical America comes a pleasant member of the nightshade family with blue starry flowers that are produced constantly all season from fall to spring. Each bloom is over an inch across. But the plant is an annual, and blooms only for one season. Don't try to hold browallia over for second winter.

LOCATION: Warm humid atmosphere. East or west window. Partial sun.

HEIGHT: Medium—up to 15 inches. Trails and spreads attractively.

SOIL: Average garden loam.

WATERING: Let soil dry between soakings.

PROPAGATION: Sprouts readily from spring-sown seed.

SPECIAL CARE: If the atmosphere is too dry, browallia is susceptible to white fly. Spray plant with a nicotine insecticide.

BURN PLANT (*Aloe vera*)

An old-time house plant, a member of the aloe family. Some of our grandmothers used the juice from the leaves to relieve burns. The saps of other varieties were used medicinally in a number of ways— one was put on a baby's thumb to prevent him from sucking it! Dense clusters of red flowers appear annually.

LOCATION: Full sun. Impervious to warm dry air.

HEIGHT: To 6 inches.

SOIL: Gritty sandy earth—containing if possible, a bit of old limestone or mortar. Perfect drainage is vital.

WATERING: Plant should be watered only every week or ten days, except when new growth appears or flowers are imminent. If foliage becomes limp, more water is needed.

PROPAGATION: By stem cuttings. To prevent rot, their ends should be touched with a hot iron before they are potted in gritty sandy soil.

BURRO'S TAIL (*Sedum morganianum*)

Blue-green foliage with a silvery cast is densely settled on long trailing stems. A beautiful and unusual plant that will do especially well in a hanging basket. Annually brilliant scarlet flowers appear at the stem tips. ▶

LOCATION: Full sun.

HEIGHT: Low; stems trail down over pot or basket a foot or more.

SOIL: Gritty, sandy garden soil.

WATERING: Only often enough to prevent the fleshy foliage from shriveling.

PROPAGATION: A four-inch stem may be broken off and potted an inch or two deep in gritty, sandy soil. It should not be overwatered lest the stem rot at the soil surface.

CACTUS (*Pereskia aculeata*)

Sometimes called Barbados gooseberry or lemon vine. Native to the hills of Mexico, the West Indies, and South America, here is an unusual cactus, whose spines are all but hidden in the leaf axils. First the leaves are green, next they turn yellow, and finally, in full sun, deep pink while the undersides are purple. Fragrant creamy white flowers open annually. If conditions suit, this plant becomes a vine and slowly climbs up the window frame.

LOCATION: Full sun.

HEIGHT: Climbs. Plant may be trimmed and pruned to fit any space desired.

SOIL: Ordinary light, sandy garden soil.

WATERING: Soil should be kept rather dry.

◀ FRAGRANCE: The scent of sweet lemons.

CACTUS (*"Cereus monstrosus"*) ▶

From the hot dry areas of Brazil comes this positively dangerous yet fascinating plant, whose scientific determination seems uncertain. The rugged green branches are guarded by myriads of ferocious spines yet the blossoms are delicate and beautiful. Pale pink flowers, each one with countless petals and a gold-and-green tufted center, appear annually.

LOCATION: Full sun.

HEIGHT: Tall.

SOIL: Gritty, sandy, gravelly soil.

WATERING: Sparingly.

FRAGRANCE: Fresh rich scent.

PROPAGATION: About six inches of one of the spiny branches may be cut off and repotted in the same type of soil, with the bottom end planted an inch or two deep. Heavy gloves should be worn and great care taken to avoid contact with the spines.

▲

CACTUS, BISHOP'S–CAP (*Astrophytum myriostigma*)

This small spineless green cactus is shaped like a bishop's cap with five definite ribs, and a jaunty golden-petaled flower atop the cap.

LOCATION: Full sun. Does beautifully in dry house or apartment air.

HEIGHT: Low, 3 to 5 inches

SOIL: Gritty, sandy, gravelly earth.

WATERING: Perhaps once a week. Its need for water may be judged by the firmness of the plant. If it seems to shrink or crease, it needs more water.

FRAGRANCE: As with most cacti, this blossom is subtly fragrant.

CACTUS (*Cereus peruvianus*) ▶

South America produces a number of varieties of Cereus cacti. In this one, the dramatic fluted branches, growing one out of another, suggest Arizona's great desert cactus, the saguaro. In California this variety grows practically to tree size indoors. In other parts of the country it is more restrained. Annually great fragrant white flowers nearly ten inches across appear.

LOCATION: Full sun.

HEIGHT: Tall.

SOIL: Gritty, sandy, gravelly earth.

WATERING: Sparingly except when in bud and bloom, then increase water supply.

FRAGRANCE: Rich tropical scent.

41

▲

CACTUS, CHRISTMAS (*Schlumbergera bridgesii*)

Pendent green branches are tipped with vivid red flowers that remain fresh for weeks on the plant. To help the plant bloom by Christmas, summer it in the garden—in its pot—or on a hot, sunny, windowsill. Water it hardly at all. Let the foliage become somewhat limp. In early September begin to water, gradually increasing the amount and frequency. Hopefully, the result will be a magnificent array of colorful flowers for the holidays.

LOCATION: Full sun. Allow plenty of space at each side.

HEIGHT: Low; trails and spreads.

SOIL: Gritty, sandy, gravelly earth.

WATERING: Less than average.

PROPAGATION: Break off a branch three to eight inches long. Bury it one or two inches deep in the soil of another pot. It will root rapidly.

◄ CACTUS, NOTOCACTUS (*Notocactus leninghausii*)

From southern Brazil comes this dome-shaped plant with slightly undulating sides and golden hairlike spines. Annually a bright yellow flower two inches across appears near the top.

LOCATION: Full sun.

HEIGHT: Low to tall, 6 inches to 3 feet—the latter after many years.

SOIL: Gritty, sandy, gravelly earth—perfect drainage.

WATERING: Should be watered lightly and sparingly.

42

CACTUS, OLD–MAN (*Cephalocereus senilis*)

A shaggy white mane of long waving "hair" tumbles down from the top of a cylindrical stem. Each year the "hair" grows thicker and longer and wavier until it become a rather enchanting tangle. Out of these tousled locks, and as a complete surprise, come two-inch rose-colored flowers. To coax any cactus into bloom,

▼

grow it in a container much too small. Let the roots be cramped and pressed tightly together. This seems brutal, but actually the plant thus grown is sure to bloom.

LOCATION: Full sun.
HEIGHT: Medium.
SOIL: Gritty, gravelly, sandy earth.
WATERING: Water sparingly.
FRAGRANCE: A sweet and elusive scent all its own.

CACTUS, ORCHID (*Epiphyllum* ▶ hybrids)

No fierce thorns on this tropical beauty, which will produce flowers often a foot across. The bloom looks something like a water lily. It is many-petaled, cornucopia-shaped, and filled with feathery stamens, and may be orange, pink, red, or white. A mature plant seldom opens fewer than half a dozen flowers at once.

LOCATION: Full sun.

HEIGHT: Medium. Will tend to become huge. It may be pruned to fit any space.

SOIL: Light, rich, sandy loam with bits of grit and gravel added.

WATERING: Soil should be kept rather dry except when plant is in bud and bloom.

FRAGRANCE: A penetrating sweet scent.

PROPAGATION: A branch six to eight inches long may be broken off and potted, with the bottom end of the stem buried about two inches under the soil. In a year or two it will become a flowering plant.

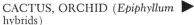

43

## CACTUS, RAT–TAIL (*Aporocactus flagelliformis*)

The half-inch-thick stems are covered with bristly hairs and spill down from an upright column, giving a gay fountain-like effect. Once a year in late winter dramatic three-inch flowers star the prickly stalks. The blossoms are firm, shiny, and thick-petaled, and each one lasts many days. They appear here and there over the plant with no apparent rhyme or reason.

LOCATION: Full sun.

HEIGHT: Medium to 1 foot.

SOIL: Gritty, gravelly, sandy earth.

WATERING: Sparingly. Once or twice a week.

FRAGRANCE: Exotic sweet scent.

PROPAGATION: A three- to five-inch stalk broken off and with one end buried an inch or two deep in the soil of another pot soon becomes a new plant.

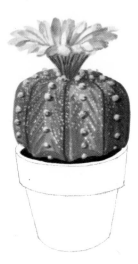

## CACTUS, SAND–DOLLAR (*Astrophytum asterias*)

From Mexico comes this small green cushion of a plant with an almost geometric pattern over its bright green surface, and rows of separate tufts of down reaching from top to bottom. Each year at the top, and directly in the center, a golden flower unfolds from a scarlet base. The flower is nearly as broad as the plant, has many petals and an open flaring shape, and lasts in bloom for several days. The plant blossoms only once a year.

LOCATION: Full sun.

HEIGHT: Low—3 to 6 inches.

SOIL: Gritty, sandy, gravelly soil. Perfect drainage needed.

WATERING: Sparingly except when flower bud appears; when water should be given until bloom fades. But soil should always remain dry a day or two between waterings.

## CALADIUM, FANCY–LEAVED

A truly glamorous foliage plant from tropical America. The leaves are of many colors, red, pink, white, green, silver and some with marbled effects. Many are veined in contrasting tints—often the same leaf displays a great variety of hues.

LOCATION: Thrives in partial shade, or filtered sun, in a temperature of 70° F. to 80° F.

HEIGHT: 1 to 1½ feet.

SOIL: A mixture of sand and average garden loam. For the best and deepest colors the soil should be acid.

WATERING: Soil should be kept moist but never soggy.

SPECIAL CARE: Toward spring the foliage begins to die back. Gradually water less. The tubers should remain bone-dry in the container for two months. About mid-August they may be repotted with fresh soil, and watered again.

## CALLA LILY (*Zantedeschia aethiopica*) ▶

In Mexico City in the great open flower markets these pure-white beauties dominate the scene for weeks around Christmastime, and off and on all winter. Callas are adaptable. They will thrive in an ordinary window garden, and they are especially becoming to contemporary houses and decor.

LOCATION: Full sun. Preferred temperature no higher than 65° F.

HEIGHT: To 3 feet.

SOIL: Richest garden loam, with well-decomposed barnyard or bagged manure added.

WATERING: Give quantities of *warm* water, especially when in bud and flower. One of the few plants that can sit in a saucer of water part of the time.

SPECIAL CARE: Plant each bulb one and one-half inches deep in a six-inch container. Set in a cool, dim-lit place for three to four weeks, then bring to full sun and give plenty of water and plant food every few days. An August potting should bloom in October. When blooms are finished, watering should be gradually stopped. Let bulb remain in container in dry soil until August, then repot with fresh earth.

45

CAMELLIA (*Camellia japonica*)

A beautiful small tree that flowers annually, and sometimes all winter, if kept at a temperature of 60° F., no higher. The flowers are firm and waxy and may be rose, red, white, or pink. Some are attractively marked with contrasting tints. If grown in too warm a place, blooms fail to develop, or buds drop. But even so, the smooth glossy leaves make it an excellent foliage plant. Summer it in the garden or on a semi-shaded windowsill.

LOCATION: Sun or part sun.

HEIGHT: To 3 feet or more.

SOIL: Rich and acid, with leaf mold added.

WATERING: Soak thoroughly, then permit to just dry before rewatering. Keep soil rather dry until November. Syringe the foliage daily the year round.

SPECIAL CARE: Fertilize every week all year with an acid plant food, oftener when in bud and bloom.

CEROPEGIA (*Ceropegia sandersonii*) ▶

A marathon climber and trailer with gray-green leaves in pairs, each pair widely separated from the next on the stem. The deep cream and green flower resembles a miniature parachute descending.

LOCATION: Filtered sunlight. East or west window.

HEIGHT: Climbs. Given a small trellis, a few stakes or lines of string, this vine will twine up a window frame.

SOIL: Rich garden loam with a little extra sand and humus.

WATERING: Less than average.

## CHENILLE PLANT (*Acalypha hispida*) ▶

Sometimes called red-hot cattail. Grows wild in the East Indies. From beneath the top leaves of this trim upright plant, foot-long scarlet "chenille" tassels trail down.

LOCATION: Sunny window, warm room.

HEIGHT: To 15 inches.

SOIL: Equal parts sandy loam and humus. Provide perfect drainage with a one-inch layer of pebbles or broken crock in the bottom of the container.

WATERING: Soil should be kept moderately moist. Spray foliage daily with clear water at room temperature.

SPECIAL CARE: Needs high humidity to be its best. Set on a tray of pebbles and water, with the bottom of the container raised above the water, as it will not tolerate sodden roots. Every spring repot in fresh soil. Prune both top and roots to keep plant from becoming ungainly and too tall for the window.

## CHINESE EVERGREEN (*Aglaonema commutatum*)

Native to Borneo and the Philippines. A tropical plant that is completely at home in the smallest, hottest, driest apartment or the largest, airiest country house, and anywhere in between. A guaranteed foolproof plant for beginners, it will even flourish in dim or artificial light, and grows well on a table beneath a lamp. Wherever you put it, it thrives.

LOCATION: Any exposure.

HEIGHT: Medium.

SOIL: Ordinary garden loam. Or it may be grown in a vase of water if you prefer.

WATERING: Should be watered thoroughly and allowed to dry before next packing.

PROPAGATION: By division as it matures.

▼

## CHINESE EVERGREEN (*Aglaonema treubii*)

A tropical plant from Asia, easy and foolproof for beginners. Graceful slim pointed leaves bluish-green and glossy with pleasantly patterned silver variations. Flowers insignificant greenish-white. May be grown in water in a clear glass vase where the roots are as attractive as the greenery. Thrives cheerfully in heat or coolness, brilliant sun or dim corners, moisture or dryness.

LOCATION: Adapts to all locations.

HEIGHT: Medium—up to 15 inches.

SOIL: Any average garden soil.

WATERING: Should be watered thoroughly and allowed to dry before next soaking.

▼

47

CLERODENDRUM (*Clerodendrum thomsoniae*)

A twining vine of great proportions that can reach the ceiling in a season. Judicious pruning keeps it within bounds. Annually and for weeks in late winter white and cherry-colored flowers poke out from rich broad green leaves.

LOCATION: Sunny windows. Ideal temperature 65° F. day and night. High humidity.

HEIGHT: Climbs. Needs string or wire to twine around.

SOIL: Rich loam.

WATERING: Soil should be kept moist in the plant's growing season, when new leaves are coming and buds forming.

SPECIAL CARE: After the blooms fade, plant should be given less water and a cooler location. If the roots seem cramped, repotting is advisable. It should be fertilized with manure monthly.

COLEUS

Sometimes called painted nettle. Member of the mint family and native to the East Indies. Myriads of shades are represented in the foliage of this gay window plant—green, yellow, red, brown, dusty pink and gold. The leaf size and shape also vary. Some are heart-shaped, some oval and many crumpled, toothed, and frilled.

LOCATION: Brilliant light, full sun for vivid colors.

HEIGHT: Best pruned to compact size and shape, perhaps 1 foot.

SOIL: Average garden loam.

WATERING: More than average.

SPECIAL CARE: Branch cuttings should be potted each spring for new plants. If kept too dry, the plant is often attacked by mealy bugs (see p. 14 for treatment).

COLEUS 'Ruffle Beauty'

Something unusual and different. Deeply scalloped and ruffled succulent leaves with lavender veins. The foliage turns from pink to red with narrow dark-green edges. More compact habit of growth than the ordinary varieties. Needs the same location and care as other varieties, but less water.

**COLUMNEA** (*Columnea microphylla*) ▶

New World jungle plant that trails attractively. Red tubular flowers appear to walk up the ladder-like foliage. May also have pink or yellow blooms, generously produced from fall until spring.

LOCATION: Filtered sunlight, east or west window. Ideal temperature 65° F. at night; 75° F. by day.

HEIGHT: Trails. Plant is lovely spilling from a hanging basket.

SOIL: Equal parts loam, humus, and sand. A one-inch layer of pebbles or broken crock for drainage.

WATERING: Soil should be kept moist, and foliage frequently sprayed.

PROPAGATION: Six-inch stem ends may be planted an inch or two deep in moist sand or vermiculite, and covered with plastic or an upside-down tumbler to increase humidity.

SPECIAL CARE: To encourage bushy growth, stem ends should be trimmed back frequently when the plant is young.

**COPPERLEAF** (*Acalypha wilkesiana*)

Often called firedragon. Brilliant scarlet foliage rivals its relative the chenille plant, and the leaves are almost as colorful— often a mixture of orange, green, white, yellow and brown.

◀ LOCATION: Filtered or full sunlight. Preferred temperature 60° F. at night, 70° F. by day. High humidity needed.

HEIGHT: To 15 inches.

SOIL: Rich garden loam with sand and humus added. Perfect drainage required.

WATERING: Soil should be kept damp but never soggy. Foliage should be sprayed daily.

PROPAGATION: New plants grow easily from leaf or stem cuttings set in sand or vermiculite.

SPECIAL CARE: Plant should *never be fed*. In spring it may be repotted with fresh soil; roots and top should be pruned to keep the plant small and compact.

◀ **CORN PLANT** (*Dracaena fragrans massangeana*)

A dramatic, tropical foliage plant whose arching leaves grow from a main central stem and resemble a miniature stalk of field corn. A rough-and-tumble variety that you simply can't discourage. Will grow in soil or water, any location or any temperature.

LOCATION: Full sun or shade.

HEIGHT: Medium to tall—15 inches to 15 feet.

SOIL: Ordinary garden earth.

WATERING: Average.

SPECIAL CARE: If the plant grows too tall and leggy, cut off the main stalk up where the leaves are full and shapely, and repot.

49

▲

CROSSANDRA (*Crossandra infundib-uliformis*)

Something new and different, and a must if you can provide ample humidity. This handsome plant with glossy gardenia-like foliage comes from the East Indies. Salmon-colored blossoms emerge from the midst of laurel-shaped leaves almost constantly. These open wide and the many layers of petals fall gracefully back.

LOCATION: Filtered sunlight, east or west window. Needs high humidity.

HEIGHT: Medium—to 15 inches.

SOIL: Rich, black garden loam, humus added.

WATERING: Keep soil wet but never soggy. Spray foliage at least daily, oftener if possible.

SPECIAL CARE: Plant pot should be set on a tray of pebbles and water, with the pot raised above the water line.

CROWN OF THORNS, CHRIST'S THORN (*Euphorbia milii*)

A weird but appealing succulent from Madagascar. Its gray branches are covered with fierce spikes, but emerald-green leaves soften the effect. The flowers, which bloom the year around except for a fall rest period, unfold in pairs at the tip of each crooked branch. Pale green at the start, they become in succession light apricot, deep pink, and finally an intense carmine.

LOCATION: Full sun preferred.

HEIGHT: Tall. Should be kept pruned to desired size.

SOIL: Gritty, sandy garden loam.

WATERING: Soil should be kept rather dry.

PROPAGATION: Six-inch branch ends may be cut off and potted, with the bottom end two inches under the soil.

SPECIAL CARE: Plant needs a fall rest period in semi-shade with very little water.

## CROTON, "SHOWER OF GOLD"
(*Codiaeum* species)

An exotic tropical plant originally from Europe. Slender, waving, ribbon-like leaves are spotted, streaked and frequently rimmed with gold and occasionally red. When new leaves first appear they are a deep green. As they age the colors develop. Although the croton will thrive in shade, it flaunts the gayest, giddiest tints in full sunlight. Summer it on the porch, in the garden, or on any open windowsill. Fresh air during the warm weather greatly improves its vigor.

LOCATION: Full sun preferred, with protection from noon glare by a curtain or other plants.

HEIGHT: Medium—to 15 inches.

SOIL: Average garden loam.

WATERING: Keep soil moist but never soggy.

PROPAGATION: Leaf cuttings readily root.

## CRINUM LILY (*Crinum bulbispermum*)

From Africa and Asia these mysterious bulbs bring their glamorous flowers to our windows. For months nothing happens; only a few lank ribbon-like leaves trail limply out of the pot. But eventually a flower stalk appears, then buds and finally blossoms. Centered in each deep-pink flower is a lovely white star.

LOCATION: Full sun.

HEIGHT: Medium to 15 inches.

SOIL: Rich garden loam with humus added.

WATERING: Average.

SPECIAL CARE: After the flowers fade, watering should be gradually stopped. In the fall, the bulb should be repotted in fresh earth. If it has small bulblets around it, these should be planted separately for new lilies.

## CYCLAMEN (*Cyclamen persicum*)

Red, pink or white blooms decorate this glamorous house plant. The curving petals of the large four-inch blossoms turn back, creating a careless, windblown effect. Your Christmas plant will bloom until April if grown in good light, in a cool spot, and watered properly.

LOCATION: Filtered sun but good light. Grow plant in a cool place, close to the window glass or where the room temperature, if possible, is 45° F. to 50° F. at night and no higher than 60° F. by day.

HEIGHT: Medium—to 15 inches.

SOIL: Rich, garden loam.

WATERING: Water copiously, but always from beneath as it is susceptible to crown rot. Never wet the foliage.

SPECIAL CARE: Feed every two weeks during the growing season and when in bud and flower. Plant is difficult to hold over, but worth trying. In the spring, water only twice a month, until the leaves come loose from the corm. Store the pot on its side in a cool shady place in the garden. In August when new leaves first appear, repot in rich soil and in a container one size larger. Sink plant in the garden and water frequently. About two weeks before frost bring it into the house.

## DARLINGTONIA (*Darlingtonia californica*)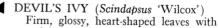

Named for the American botanist, William Darlington, this plant is native to the mountain swamps from Oregon to California. The hooded pitcher has a curious crimson-and-green tonguelike appendage which snares insects, and a sticky fluid within digests them. Solitary flowers, yellow or purple, develop best in partial shade. In autumn the leaves fall but more soon grow.

LOCATION: Filtered sunlight, east window. Cool temperature.

HEIGHT: Tall.

SOIL: Rich mixture of peat moss, sand, and sphagnum moss.

WATERING: Soil should be kept moist at all times.

## DEVIL'S IVY (*Scindapsus* 'Wilcox')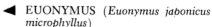

Firm, glossy, heart-shaped leaves with graceful pointed tips and dashes of yellow. A charming trailer and climber as lovely as any ivy or philodendron.

LOCATION: Thrives in any exposure. Yellow leaf streaks are brighter in a south window. Preferred temperature 60° F. to 70° F.

HEIGHT: Climbs and trails.

SOIL: Average garden earth with humus added. Several lumps of charcoal from the fireplace are welcome. One of the few plants that will grow in a container with no drainage hole.

WATERING: Soil should be kept rather dry.

PROPAGATION: From cuttings from new branch ends.

SPECIAL CARE: If leaves around the base drop, the growing ends should be pinched back. Plant needs weekly feeding.

## EUONYMUS (*Euonymus japonicus microphyllus*)

A small house-plant version of the outdoor shrub. Tiny white-edged leaves and bushy growth habits delight the window gardener. Benefits from summers in the garden in a partially shady spot. Repot in fresh soil each fall, pruning roots as well as branches to prevent legginess and keep the plant compact and shapely.

LOCATION: Filtered sunlight, east or west window. Temperature 60° F. or less.

HEIGHT: Low—to 1 foot.

SOIL: Average garden loam.

WATERING: Water thoroughly, let dry before soaking again.

ECHEVERIA (*Echeveria glauca*)

Sometimes called hen-and-chickens. This succulent plant is easy to grow, and its manner of growth has great appeal. Each large rosette of blue-green leaves, like a mother hen, guards smaller ones that cluster around it. Annually pink, coral-red, or orange flowers appear.

LOCATION: Full sun. Benefits from summering in a hot, dry, sandy garden spot.

HEIGHT: Low—to 4 inches.

SOIL: Gritty, gravelly, sandy earth.

WATERING: Only enough to keep plant from shriveling. A little more when flower buds and new growth appear.

FRAGRANCE: Flowers are sweetly scented.

PROPAGATION: Small rosettes may be cut off and potted separately.

DUMB CANE (*Dieffenbachia maculata*)

Sometimes called mother-in-law plant, because a piece of the stem, if placed on the tongue or chewed, actually renders a person speechless for a short while. This handsome tropical plant, whose upright oval leaves are a blend of ivory, green and yellow, is not otherwise poisonous.

LOCATION: Prefers a temperature of at least 70° F. and two or three hours of sun daily, but will grow well even in a north window. Benefits from high humidity.

HEIGHT: 18 to 30 inches.

SOIL: Average garden loam. Will grow a while in water, but not indefinitely.

WATERING: Soil should be allowed to dry between soakings.

PROPAGATION: Cuttings root rapidly.

53

▲

### FALSE HOLLY; CHINESE HOLLY
(*Osmanthus ilicifolius variegatus*)

This delightful house plant is no relation to the true holly, but it's a splendid substitute. The crisp leaf is smaller, slashed and spiked. Each one has a rim of white, pink-tinted when first open.

LOCATION: Filtered sunlight. Cool room. 45° F. to 60° F. Full shade in summer.

HEIGHT: Medium—to 15 inches.

SOIL: Average garden loam with sand, peat moss, and leaf mold added.

WATERING: Soil should be kept moist but never soggy.

◄ EUPHORBIA (*Euphorbia lactea*)

A cactus-like succulent spurge from the East Indies with heavy spines. The branching treelike plant has many arms all reaching upward like candelabra. New growth is lighter in hue, giving each plant two tones of green at one time. A streaked white band marks the center of every branch.

LOCATION: Full sun.

HEIGHT: Tall.

SOIL: Gritty, sandy, gravelly earth.

WATERING: Soil should remain completely dry for days, then be watered lightly.

PROPAGATION: A branch may be cut off and potted separately. Extra thick gloves are required for this operation.

FAN IRIS (*Neomarica northiana*)

Native to the jungles of Brazil. Sword-shaped leaves grow in the form of a fan. Usually there are twelve—hence its other name, apostle plant. The fragrant white flowers, resembling a cross between an orchid and an iris, are nearly four inches across and touched with violet.

LOCATION: Good light and full sun.

HEIGHT: To 2 feet.

SOIL: Average garden loam in a pot small enough to cramp the roots.

WATERING: Needs copious watering, and should be sprayed daily with water at room temperature.

FRAGRANCE: Delicate and sweet.

PROPAGATION: Plantlets from the flowering stem may be potted separately.

## GENERAL CARE OF FERNS

LOCATION: Filtered sunshine, or none, but good light needed. East or west window ideal.

SOIL: All ferns have fine roots and need loose soil easy to penetrate. Equal parts humus, loam and sand, and if possible, some leaf mold and a little charcoal. Perfect drainage is vital.

WATERING: Soak daily, and mist-spray foliage one or more times each day. High humidity is essential.

PROPAGATION: Divide roots when repotting. Or cut off side runners, wind these up and bury a half-inch deep.

SPECIAL CARE: Repot annually in fresh soil. Summer in a protected garden spot or shady window, and water abundantly. If the leaves turn yellow, plant may need less sun, more plant food, more watering or more spraying.

FERN, BIRD'S-NEST (*Asplenium* ▶ *nidus*)

When new fronds first appear deep in the heart of the plant, and before they uncurl, they are solid ovals resembling a bird's eggs in the nest.

▲

FERN, BOSTON (*Nephrolepis exaltata
'Bostoniensis'*)

This old-time favorite is still a desirable
house plant. But if it becomes immense
and shaggy, harden your heart and discard
it, first making some new plants from the
wiry runners at the fern's base.

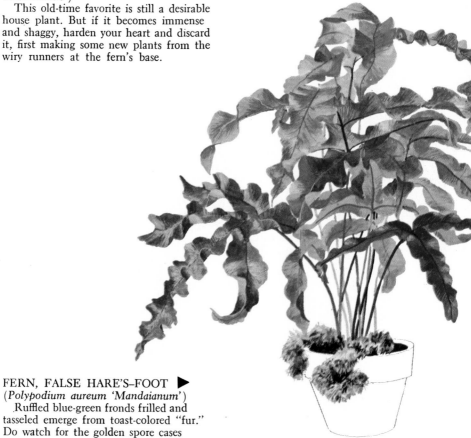

FERN, FALSE HARE'S–FOOT ▶
(*Polypodium aureum 'Mandaianum'*)

.Ruffled blue-green fronds frilled and
tasseled emerge from toast-colored "fur."
Do watch for the golden spore cases
which appear on the undersides of the
leaves. To propagate, break off one of the
"feet" and pot separately.

FERN, HOLLY (*Cyrtomium falcatum* ▶
'*Rochefordianum compactum*')
The shiny, spiked and slashed foliage
suggests the familiar Christmas holly. This
one is particularly adaptable to city
windows because it thrives with less
humidity and in a hotter atmosphere than
most ferns.

◀ FERN, LACE (*Nephrolepis exaltata*
'*Whitmannii*')
A variety related to the Boston fern
but with lacier fronds. These tend to
revert to the coarse Boston type. Trim
off the rebel fronds as they appear.

FERN, MAIDENHAIR (*Adiantum* ▶
*tenerum* '*Wrightii*')
Less easy than other ferns, but well
worth a try for the great charm of its
wiry black stems and ruffled lacy fronds.
A temperature of 65° F. or below is preferred. Plenty of humidity needed. Occasionally the plant rests and loses its
greenery. Don't worry, more fronds soon
appear.

57

**FERN, MOTHER** (*Asplenium bulbiferum*)

Grows wild from Malaya to New Zealand, and adapts to a broad range of temperatures indoors. Another fragile lacy variety which grows small fernlets on the fronds. Watch for the nearly invisible bulbils and pot them for new plants.

**FERN, RABBIT'S–FOOT** (*Davallia canariensis*)

From out of the furry "feet" casual windblown fronds grow. Break off a "foot" and repot and soon a new plant will develop.

**FERN, SILVER–LACE** (*Pteris argyraea*)

*Pteris* derives from the Greek word for "feather" and refers to the light, airy quality of the foliage. These broad silver fronds are edged with green. Notice the interesting spore cases that appear beneath the rolled edges—on this and other ferns. Don't mistake them for scale insects.

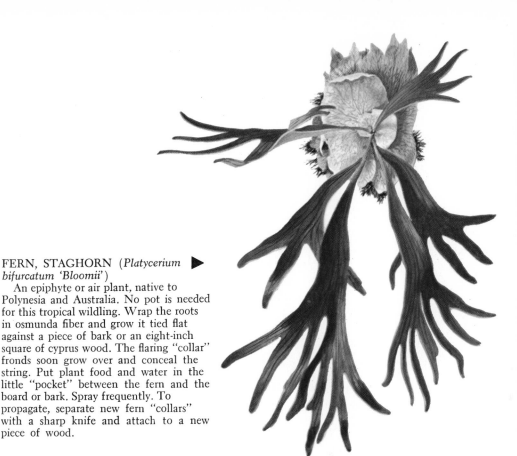

FERN, STAGHORN (*Platycerium* ▶
*bifurcatum 'Bloomii'*)

An epiphyte or air plant, native to
Polynesia and Australia. No pot is needed
for this tropical wildling. Wrap the roots
in osmunda fiber and grow it tied flat
against a piece of bark or an eight-inch
square of cyprus wood. The flaring "collar"
fronds soon grow over and conceal the
string. Put plant food and water in the
little "pocket" between the fern and the
board or bark. Spray frequently. To
propagate, separate new fern "collars"
with a sharp knife and attach to a new
piece of wood.

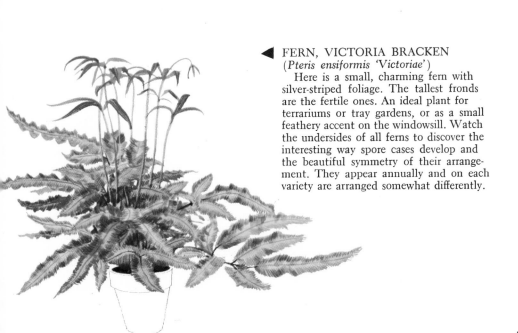

◀ FERN, VICTORIA BRACKEN
(*Pteris ensiformis 'Victoriae'*)

Here is a small, charming fern with
silver-striped foliage. The tallest fronds
are the fertile ones. An ideal plant for
terrariums or tray gardens, or as a small
feathery accent on the windowsill. Watch
the undersides of all ferns to discover the
interesting way spore cases develop and
the beautiful symmetry of their arrange-
ment. They appear annually and on each
variety are arranged somewhat differently.

### FIG, CLIMBING VARIEGATED (*Ficus radicans* '*Variegata*')

A tropical member of the mulberry family. The short two-inch green-and-white leaves are pointed, and no two patterned alike. Branching stems make this a fine climber or trailer. Flourishes in a hanging basket or on the window-garden shelf. Excellent for an all-green garden where the appealing sage-tinted foliage contrasts delightfully with other plants.

LOCATION: Filtered sunlight, east or west window, or south if shaded by other plants.

HEIGHT: Climbs and trails.

SOIL: Ordinary soil from the garden.

WATERING: More than average. Soil should be kept slightly damp most of the time but about once a week should be allowed to dry between waterings.

### FIG, FIDDLE–LEAF (*Ficus lyrata*)

Most sweet-tempered of house plants and one that flourishes on an abundance of neglect! Large rich green leaves are interestingly patterned with deep veins. Each has a glossy surface, slightly ruffled edges and is irregular in form.

LOCATION: South, east, or west exposure, or even an interior location if there is ample light.

HEIGHT: Tall—from 3 to 10 feet in a ten-inch pot.

SOIL: Ordinary garden loam. Plant need not be repotted until roots emerge from the bottom hole of the container.

WATERING: Soil should remain dry two or three days between soakings.

SPECIAL CARE: The broad shiny leaves should be occasionally sponged off with soap and water, to remove house dust.

▲

FIG, CREEPING (*Ficus pumila*)
A somewhat rare but easy-to-grow plant from tropical Asia. This enthusiastic climber runs up walls, clinging with aerial roots to even a painted surface. While it climbs, small heart-shaped leaves develop close to the main stem. Suddenly, when mature, attractive huge leaves three or four times the size of the original ones appear, an entirely different kind of growth! Here is a vine that no insect relishes, that any kind of soil pleases, and that even a good freeze won't discourage.
LOCATION: East or west window. Average house temperature.
HEIGHT: Climbs and trails.
SOIL: Ordinary loam from the garden.
WATERING: Soil should be kept moist, and tops should be sprayed daily or oftener. Surprisingly the mist spray encourages the vine to cling.

FIG, MISTLETOE (*Ficus diversifolia*) ▶
From Malaya. As tough and durable as all the figs. Each waxy, two-inch leaf is attractively veined and shaped like a raindrop. Along the branches near every leaf axil appears a small red fig, and often a pair. These last months on the plant. Prune to keep desired shape and height.
LOCATION: East or west window, an interior location with plenty of light.
HEIGHT: Medium—to 18 inches.
SOIL: Ordinary garden loam.
WATERING: More than average. Keep damp most of the time, but once every ten days or so let soil dry between waterings.

61

## FINGER ARALIA (*Dizygotheca* ▶ *elegantissima*)

A plant of grace and elegance. Narrow, ribbon-like, notched leaves of dark green are borne in groups of seven to eleven on slim stems. Prune branch tips drastically from time to time to prevent the foliage from thinning at the bottom. Grows fast.

LOCATION: Warm room, high humidity, partial sun. A west window ideal.

HEIGHT: Tall. Keep pruned to 18 inches.

SOIL: Ordinary garden loam.

WATERING: Keep damp but never soggy.

SPECIAL CARE: If you have an ailing aralia, summer it in a protected, semishady spot in the garden. Remove from the pot and set in the earth after all frost danger has passed. Cut the top back to four inches. Keep watered and fed all summer.

▲

## FINGERNAIL PLANT (*Neoregelia spectabilis*)

A bromeliad, and a highly ornamental member of the pineapple family. Leaf tips are tinted as if with red fingernail polish, and the plant heart is also brilliant crimson. If possible collect rain water for this fastidious aristocrat because it languishes with water that is too acid or too alkaline.

LOCATION: East or west window preferred. South window if shaded by other plants. Needs two or three hours of sun daily or the vivid leaf markings grow pale. Ideal temperature 50° F. at night, 70° F. by day.

HEIGHT: Tall—to 2 feet.

SOIL: Equal parts osmunda fiber, sharp sand, and ordinary earth. Pebbles or broken crock in the bottom for drainage.

WATERING: Keep water always in vase-like plant center, and soil slightly damp but never soaking-wet. Mist-spray biweekly.

PROPAGATION: Break or cut apart offshoot leaves from around the base of the plant. Pot in osmunda fiber.

**FLAMINGO FLOWER** (*Jacobinia* ▶
*suberecta*)

From Brazil comes a rapid-growing
tropical beauty with light-green velvety
leaves and clusters of upright coral flowers
at the branch tips. Blossoms riotously and
for a long period of time if the air is
high in humidity, but is apt to straggle
and pine in a dry atmosphere. Mist-spray
several times a day, set the pot on a tray
of pebbles and water, and you may well
succeed. The lovely blooms are quite
worth the extra effort.

LOCATION: Full sunlight, or east or
west window. Keep temperature at 65° F.
or above and provide high humidity.

HEIGHT: Low—to 1 foot.

SOIL: Rich garden loam with leaf mold
added.

WATERING: Keep moist but not soggy.
Spray foliage many times daily.


**FLOWERING MAPLE; CHINESE** ▶
**BELLFLOWER** (*Abutilon hybridium*)

A charming, small "maple" tree for
your window garden. Pink, red, yellow,
apricot, or white flowers like old-fashioned
hoop petticoats swing under the foliage
almost all winter. The white-rimmed leaves
are shaped like those of the maple. Trim
branch tips to keep blooming. Give no
food lest the plant run to foliage instead
of blossoms. For best performance keep
pot-bound.

LOCATION: Cool window. If possible a
temperature of 60° F. Full sun. South or
west exposure.

HEIGHT: Tall, but keep pruned to 18
inches, or it grows leggy.

SOIL: Average garden loam.

WATERING: Fairly moist, but never
allow water to remain in the saucer.

PROPAGATION: Cut branch tips four to
six inches long. Set one to two inches deep
in moist sand or vermiculite.

## FUCHSIA, LADY'S–EARDROPS
(*Fuchsia magellanica gracilis*)

Named for Leonard Fuchs, a German doctor and ardent botanist of the sixteenth century. Bewitching two-toned pendent flowers in colors that include pinks, magentas, violets, and white. If conditions please this lovely plant, it blossoms for weeks, beginning in late winter. Difficult for city apartments, but nothing is impossible!

LOCATION: A cool part of the window. Shield from full sun. Preferred temperature 60° F. to 65° F.

HEIGHT: Medium—keep pruned to 18 inches.

SOIL: Rich garden loam with a handful of humus and manure added per pot.

WATERING: Keep roots constantly moist and tops frequently sprayed.

SPECIAL CARE: A pinch of soot from your fireplace chimney on the soil deepens the flower tones. In October and November water less, cut some of the top growth back and repot in a container one size larger, or root-prune as well and use same size container. Allow to rest until January in a cool place 50° F. to 60° F. at night. Then give ample water, a daily foliage spray and weekly food. Fuchsias are susceptible to white fly. Examine a new plant carefully before purchasing it.

## GARDENIA (*Gardenia jasminoides*)

Named after another physician who chose gardening for his leisure moments, Dr. Alexander Garden of Charleston, South Carolina, this beautiful plant is a challenge to the green-thumbed window gardener.

LOCATION: Ideal conditions include full sun in winter, shade in summer, high humidity and a temperature of 60° F. at night, 70° F. by day.

HEIGHT: Tall—to 3 feet.

SOIL: Well-drained, rich, acid soil. Feed aluminum sulphate to keep the soil acid.

WATERING: Syringe the leaves daily. Never let the soil dry completely. If buds drop, the air is too dry.

PROPAGATION: Trimmed branches will root in water, sand, or vermiculite.

SPECIAL CARE: Repot with fresh soil in the spring and, if possible, summer plant in the garden, sinking the container in the earth. Nip off all buds that appear, to encourage winter blooming. Weekly during the winter submerge the pot to the brim in a pail of water and leave until the top of the soil feels damp.

LOCATION: Full sun, preferably a south window.

HEIGHT: From 15 inches to several feet. Prune to keep shape and height desired.

SOIL: Average garden earth, not rich lest it produce lush foliage and no bloom. Do not fertilize.

WATERING: Spray foliage once or twice a week, but keep pot soil rather dry, letting it remain dry for two days between waterings.

PROPAGATION: Six-inch stems trimmed off will root if placed in a separate pot of earth and kept rather dry until new growth appears. Cuttings taken in the spring should become healthy plants by fall and ready for a winter of flowering.

SPECIAL CARE: In order to bloom, geraniums must be pot-bound. Keep faded blossoms picked off. If desired, remove from the pot and grow loose in the garden all summer, picking off any buds that form. In the fall repot in fresh earth. Or cut off and plant all the six-inch' thriving ends of the leafiest branches, and discard the parent plant.

To MAKE A TREE GERANIUM: Select a plant with a straight main stalk. Trim off all side branches. Insert a stake in the pot and tie the plant to this. Permit no more than five leaves at a time to grow at the top and no flowers at all. As new leaves appear, cut off bottom ones. It takes about two years to make a 3-foot tree geranium. When it is the height desired, allow a bush of foliage and flowers to develop at the top of the stalk.

▲

GERANIUM, APPLE, NUTMEG, CINNAMON (*Pelargonium* species)

These geraniums form an ideal background for other plants. Although they do bloom, it is for the spicy aroma and general appeal of their foliage that we grow them. Add a leaf of any of the above to applesauce. Dry the foliage and use in sachets. Toss a few fresh leaves into the bath water.

GERANIUM, COMMON RED ▶
VARIETIES

Of all our house plants, the ordinary, common geranium is one that everyone knows. Red, pink and white ones have bloomed in windows for hundreds of years. The plant makes only a few demands but those in loud tones. In order to flower it must have its roots cramped out of all reason.

GERANIUM (*Pelargonium* 'Dr. Living-ston') ▶

Grown mainly for the foliage although the delicate lavender flowers also have their charm. This geranium makes a fine backdrop for other blossoming plants. The skeleton-like leaves bring contrasting form and texture to the window. Crushed foliage emits a lemon scent.

◀ GERANIUM (*Pelargonium* 'French Lace')

Ruffled frothy leaves with white margins give this plant its name. Makes wonderful sachets and adds a pungent scent to potpourris.

◀ GERANIUM, IVY (*Pelargonium peltatum* 'Willy')

Light-green leaves appear as if cut and folded from heavy wax paper. Their many pointed tips and glossy surface add to their appeal. This is a plant that trails and does well on a shelf across the window, or in a basket. Vivid flowers scarcely stop coming from fall to spring.

GERANIUM, IVY (*Pelargonium*
'l'Élégante,' also known as 'Sunset')
Tiny new ivy-shaped leaves unfold at
first pure white and waxlike. When these
increase in size, they become like the
mature leaves, green with white rims.
When this graceful trailing plant is grown
in full sun and kept somewhat dry, the
rims of the leaves turn shocking pink.

GERANIUM, MINIATURE (*Pelar-*
*gonium hortorum* 'Pigmy')
Scarlet flowers appear when the plant
is only four inches high. An ideal plant
where space is at a premium. Half a
dozen, in different colors (they come in
pink and white too) make a complete
miniature garden on a tray.

GERANIUM, PEPPERMINT (*Pelar-*
*gonium tomentosum*)
These large, soft, velvety green leaves
are covered with silver down and pleasant
to touch. Water drops turn silver and
bounce off the foliage in an enchanting
manner. Here is a leaf that also lends a
special tang to the applesauce.

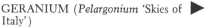

GERANIUM, ROSE (*Pelargonium graveolens*)

The frilled and ruffled foliage is a special delight to look at, to touch and to smell. Wonderful dried in potpourris. Or put a small new leaf in the empty jelly jar just ahead of the jelly.

GERANIUM (*Pelargonium* 'Skies of Italy')

The foliage of this geranium is nearly as vivid as the rich red blossoms. Maple-shaped leaves are edged creamy white. A brown zone in the center is splashed red and orange. In full sun foliage colors are their most brilliant.

HONEY BELLS (*Mahernia verticillata*)

Fragrant clusters of small golden bells appear among the trailing stems of fern-like foliage. Give semi-shade in an east or west window during its summer rest period.

LOCATION: Full sun, south window.

HEIGHT: Climbs and trails; give ample space horizontally.

SOIL: Ordinary garden loam.

WATERING: More than average.

FRAGRANCE: Blossoms smell like wild-flower honey.

PROPAGATION: Readily from stem cuttings. Bury the bottom end of each four- to six-inch cutting two inches in earth, damp sand or vermiculite.

GERMAN IVY, WATER IVY, ▶
PARLOR IVY (*Senecio mikanioides*)

An old-fashioned climbing plant from
South Africa. The starry, deep-green
leaves are somewhat like those of the
English ivy, but more fragile. The stems
have a fleshy quality, and in winter small
yellow flowers appear among them. Easy
to raise and a rapid grower.

LOCATION: Ideal temperature 50° F. to
60° F. Full sun in winter, partial shade in
summer. Too delicate to summer in the
garden.

SOIL: Ordinary garden loam.

WATERING: Soil should be allowed to
dry between soakings.

PROPAGATION: In winter cuttings from
the ends of the stems will readily root in
wet sand or water.

▲

GLOXINIA (*Sinningia speciosa*)

Originally from Brazil and a distant
relative of the African violet. Flowers of
a velvety texture, five inches across, are
in shades of pink, violet, purple, and
crimson. Some types have frilled, ruffled,
striped, and variegated blooms.

LOCATION: East or west window. Preferred temperature 70° F. Provide ample
humidity.

HEIGHT: Low—to 1 foot.

SOIL: Average garden loam with a
handful of sand and one of peat moss per
pot.

WATERING: Water thoroughly. Permit
to become almost dry, then soak again.
Keep water away from the furry leaves.

PROPAGATION: Plant tubers in January,
one to a six-inch pot, the rounded part
down. Leave a quarter of the tuber above
the soil. Water regularly. In a month or
more look for buds. The plant will flower
continuously into the spring. Rest in the
garden or in a semi-shaded window until
September. Then replace it in its usual
position and water. Should flower in
October.

GRAPE IVY (*Cissus rhombifolia*)

From South America comes this decorative, climbing and trailing plant.
Extremely adaptable, it thrives in heat or
coolness and in any location. Also resists
insects. Glossy green leaflets develop in
groups of three. The young tendrils are
reddish and "fur"-covered when they first
uncurl.

LOCATION: The more light the better,
but will grow anywhere with or without
sun.

HEIGHT: Trails and climbs.

SOIL: Average garden loam, with humus
added.

WATERING: More than average—about
every ten days pot soil should be allowed
to become quite dry to touch before
rewatering.

PROPAGATION: At annual spring repotting time the roots readily separate, and
a new plant may be made of each.

SPECIAL CARE: Susceptible to mealy
bugs. A frequent foliage spray of clear
cold water often eliminates them.

▼

HIBISCUS (*Hibiscus rosa-sinensis*)

The Hawaii state flower (though it originated in China), hibiscus comes in many variations and varieties. Basically an outdoor bush, indoors it is a slow-growing pot plant with leaves splashed green, pink and white and with spectacular red blooms, each like a hollyhock, which appear in late summer and fall.

LOCATION: Full sun. South window. Ample space horizontally and vertically.

HEIGHT: Tall—to 2 feet or more.

SOIL: Ordinary garden loam, with a handful of humus per pot.

WATERING: Soil should be allowed to dry between soakings except when plant is in bud and bloom; then it must be watered copiously and regularly, and the soil never permitted to dry completely.

SPECIAL CARE: Should be fed weekly when in bud and flower. When repotted in the spring, roots and top may be pruned if necessary, to keep plant within bounds. Benefits from a summer in the garden in a semishady spot, or on a shady window-sill.

INCH PLANT, GIANT WHITE ▶
(*Tradescantia albiflora 'Albovittata'*)

Large, bright, blue-green leaves, oval, pointed at the tips, and striped white. To keep compact and bushy turn a few of the stem ends back into the pot and anchor with hairpins. These will root and refill the plant center with fresh growth.

LOCATION: Filtered sun, full sun. Splendid in a hanging basket.

HEIGHT: A small plant that trails and climbs but needs but little space.

SOIL: Ordinary garden earth. Will grow in water for two months or so.

WATERING: Keep soil rather dry. Soak and then let the soil dry and remain so a day or two before rewatering.

PROPAGATION: Four- to six-inch stem cuttings root easily.

IVY (*Hedera helix* 'Pittsburgh') ▶

A small-leaved, trailing vine with rhythmic, curving stems. This variety is easy to raise; watch it spread its living green through your window all winter. Pale, waxy new leaflets start out diminutive, crooknecked, and composed of tiny three-fingered sunshades that straighten out into regular leaves.

LOCATION: Sun, filtered sun, or no sun.

HEIGHT: Climbs and trails—takes up very little space horizontally or vertically.

SOIL: Ordinary earth directly from the garden.

WATERING: Soak thoroughly, let dry and remain so a day or two before watering. Every week or two spray the foliage with lukewarm water.

PROPAGATION: Stem cuttings four to six inches long will grow readily. Pot these separately, burying the cut end an inch or two beneath the soil.

IVY, FEATHER (*Hedera helix* 'Meagheri')

◀ One of the smallest leaf forms, deeply cut, feathered and frothy. This variety thrives in any exposure. A fine subject for tray gardens and terrariums where the diminutive leaves help create the magic of a miniature woodland dell.

LOCATION: No sun or filtered sun. North, east, or west exposure.

HEIGHT: Small, and takes but little space horizontally or vertically. Climbs and trails.

SOIL: Ordinary garden soil.

WATERING: Soil should be allowed to dry thoroughly between waterings.

PROPAGATION: Four-inch stem cuttings will root in a few weeks in moist sand, vermiculite or water.

IVY, GLACIER (*Hedera helix* 'Glacier')

Small leaves with narrow white edges. Each looks as if an irregular-shaped leaf of green had been appliqued onto a larger one of white. Grows anywhere with good light, in sun or shade.

LOCATION: Filtered sunlight, east, west or even north window. Prefers a cool spot.

HEIGHT: Climbs and trails—needs ample space.

SOIL: Regular garden loam.

WATERING: A little more than average. Soil should be kept slightly moist except once every couple of weeks, when the earth should be allowed to dry thoroughly before it is rewatered. Foliage needs frequent spraying.

PROPAGATION: Six-inch stem cuttings root easily in damp sand, water, or ordinary soil.

71

## JESSAMINE, WILLOW–LEAVED, NIGHT–BLOOMING (*Cestrum parqui*)

Willow-like bright-green leaves are graceful and trailing. Annually, in mid-winter, richly fragrant greenish-white flowers open. For many a night they fill the house with their perfume.

LOCATION: Filtered sun, or no sun *if* you provide excellent and ample humidity and good light. A day and night temperature of 70° F. is ideal.

HEIGHT: Medium—to about 18 inches.

SOIL: Ordinary garden soil.

WATERING: Let the pot soil dry completely between soakings.

FRAGRANCE: Fresh sweet penetrating scent.

## JADE PLANT; FRIENDSHIP PLANT; JAPANESE RUBBER PLANT; JAPANESE LAUREL (*Crassula arborescens*)

A tough and indestructible South African succulent. Grows into a miniature tree with a brown trunk and branches, and thick green foliage. If grown in full sun the rims of the fleshy, rounded leaves turn red. After the plant is mature, when six to eight years old, and 2 or more feet tall, it flowers in a mist of lacy white and fragrant blossoms.

LOCATION: Full sun, with shade for three hours at midday; west window preferred. Should be summered in partial shade but never in the garden.

HEIGHT: Tall—3 to 5 feet. Can be kept pruned to 2 feet and the cuttings potted for extra plants.

SOIL: Gritty, sandy, garden loam with a little humus and gravel added.

WATERING: The soil should be allowed to remain dry for several days between soakings.

PROPAGATION: Stems four to six inches long will root in sandy, gritty soil.

SPECIAL CARE: Should be repotted in May every three or four years, but some of the surface soil should be replaced annually with fresh earth. Needs fertilizing whenever it puts forth new growths and flower buds.

## JERUSALEM CHERRY, CHRISTMAS CHERRY (*Solanum pseudo-capsicum*)

This small bushlike house plant is gay for weeks with bright red or orange berries. Benefits from a summer in the garden. Repot in the spring and prune back for an abundance of berries the following season. Warn the children, however, these fruits are poisonous to eat.

LOCATION: Full sun, filtered sun. Ideal temperature 50° F. to 60° F. High humidity needed.

HEIGHT: Medium to tall—eventually to 4 feet, unless pruned to keep smaller and more manageable.

SOIL: Ordinary loam.

WATERING: This plant must never, never be allowed to dry. Keep the soil always slightly moist, and spray the foliage daily.

◀ JASMINE, STAR (*Trachelospermum jasminoides*)

A tall woody Chinese vine with firm substantial foliage. Heavy-textured starry white flowers appear when the plant is small and young and unfold continually all fall and into the winter. Summer in the garden if possible, but keep in the pot. This rapid grower gets quite out of hand when planted loose in the earth.

LOCATION: South window. Average house temperature suits it very well.

HEIGHT: Will climb 3 or 4 feet on strings or a trellis. Keep pruned to fit your space.

SOIL: Rich garden loam.

WATERING: Let the soil dry between soakings.

FRAGRANCE: A sweet and lingering tropical scent.

KALANCHOE; BRILLIANT STAR; SCARLET GNOME (*Kalanchoe blossfeldiana*)

An easy and attractive succulent from Madagascar. Vivid red, stiff and waxy blossoms appear annually in flat-headed clusters and remain bright and fresh all winter.

LOCATION: Full sun or semi-shade. Flourishes in a hot, dry part of the window garden.

HEIGHT: Medium—to 15 inches

SOIL: Gritty, gravelly soil with a little humus added.

WATERING: Soil should be allowed to remain dry for two or three days between waterings. Needs more water when in bud and flower.

PROPAGATION: Easy to reproduce from cuttings.

SPECIAL CARE: Tops should be severely pruned back after flowers fade in the spring. Plant should rest with almost no water in a shady window or protected garden spot. In September it should be brought to the sunny window and watered regularly.

KALANCHOE (*Kalanchoe daigremontiana*)

An appealing succulent which probably originated in Madagascar. Grown widely in Florida. Propagates when small plantlets with fine hairlike roots develop along the leaf rims and drop down onto any soil below, sometimes into neighboring pots as well as their own. Here they take root and grow. The mature plant produces pink or red flowers.

LOCATION: Full sun, partial sun.

HEIGHT: Medium—to 18 inches.

SOIL: Gritty, gravelly, garden loam with sand added.

WATERING: Soil should be allowed to dry between soakings.

▼

▼

## KANGAROO VINE (*Cissus antarctica*)

Native to Australia, the land of kangaroos, this graceful climber gallops up your window fairly rapidly. A foolproof, bugproof plant that grows in any exposure, and is just as flamboyant in a north window with no sun as in a south window with streaming sun. Shiny, saw-edged leaves are covered with red "fur" when newly unfolding.

LOCATION: North, south, east or west exposure. Provide a string or trellis for the twining ends to cling to.

HEIGHT: In due time this vine will reach your ceiling, but it also may be pruned to any height desired.

SOIL: Thrives in regular garden loam.

WATERING: Average watering—soak, allow to dry, and water again.

▼

## LADYFINGER BANANA (*Musa* ▶ *cavendishii*)

A small-scale variety of the tropical banana plants with their fringed trailing leaves and exotic flowers. Will grow in a sunny, glassed-in porch, conservatory or greenhouse, and perhaps even in the house. May produce delicious, small yellow fruits if conditions suit. The large buds roll back successive purple bracts, one for each hand of bananas.

LOCATION: Full sun. Temperature no cooler than 60° F. Benefits from a summer in the garden.

HEIGHT: Tall.

SOIL: Rich earth with humus and decomposed manure added. Give ample root room in a large container.

WATERING: Water copiously, especially when in bud and when fruiting.

PROPAGATION: After the fruit has ripened, destroy the old plant and begin anew. Young shoots spring to life around the base of the parent stalk. Pot these separately.

75

## LEMON, AMERICAN WONDER
(*Citrus limonia* 'Ponderosa')

Fragrant, waxy, white flowers and huge green fruit develop at the same time and appear almost continually the year round. The fruit is large, a single lemon sometimes weighing two pounds.

LOCATION: Full sun, a south window. Won't produce flowers or fruit in an east or west window.

HEIGHT: Tall—to 4 feet. Should be grown in a redwood tub. Will develop blooms and fruit when 1½ feet high.

SOIL: Rich garden loam with humus and manure added.

FRAGRANCE: The scent resembles that of the orange blossom.

PROPAGATION: Grows rapidly from its own seed and in a few years will blossom and fruit. Each fruiting arm should be supported with a forked stick as the lemon gains in weight and size. Should be summered in the garden, if possible.

## KENTIA PALM, FAN PALM, PARADISE PALM (*Howeia forsteriana*)

A graceful and airy tropical plant. Delights in a summer on the porch or covered terrace. A rampant grower. In order to keep to proper size, repot annually in fresh soil and prune off about one-quarter of the roots at the same time. Also trim a number of top branches as well, to maintain a proper balance.

LOCATION: Filtered sun, full sun, and for a few weeks at a time it will thrive in no sun. Grow in a large wooden tub.

HEIGHT: Tall, but may be kept to 2 or 3 feet.

SOIL: Rich garden loam with a handful of dried manure and humus added.

WATERING: Keep the earth perpetually moist but never soggy.

SPECIAL CARE: Sponge off or spray foliage every few days to provide humidity, dispose of house dust, and ward off insects.

## LEOPARD PLANT (*Ligularia kaempferi* 'Aureo-maculata')

An old-time window-garden plant popular in Japan. The rounded, glossy leaves have slightly scalloped edges and are as spotted as their name indicates. The spots are a pure gold that glitters in a beam of sunlight. In midsummer the plant is ornamented with gay yellow flowers to match the leaf shade. Summers best on the windowsill, not on the porch or terrace or in the garden.

LOCATION: Filtered sunlight. South window in the winter with protection from the hot noon sun. East or west window in summer. Adapts to a temperature from 55° F. to 70° F.

HEIGHT: Low-growing—to 15 inches.

SOIL: Regular garden earth.

WATERING: Soil should be kept moist but never soggy.

PROPAGATION: In the spring the plant may be divided gently by hand where the roots tend to separate.

▲

LANTANA (*Lantana montevidensis*)

Grows wild in the mountain regions of Venezuela and Colombia where it probably originated. Thrives in a hanging basket where it spreads and trails and creates a fountain-like effect. The whole appearance is one of lacy sheets of color. Prune off straggly stems regularly to keep in flower all winter. May also be trimmed and trained into an upright bush or even espaliered.

LOCATION: Abundant sun, south or southwest window. Give ample space at each side. Preferred temperature 60° F.

HEIGHT: Trails, or makes a medium-sized bush.

SOIL: Regular garden loam.

WATERING: Water thoroughly, permit to dry, and soak again.

FRAGRANCE: Leaves are scented and in warm sun their pungent odor is evident several feet away.

PROPAGATION: Make six-inch cuttings in the spring. Set in pots in a mixture of half sand and half peat moss. Place in semi-shade in the window or in the garden until fall, pinch off any buds that form, then bring into the house for its winter flowering season.

LILY, KAFFIR (*Clivia miniata*)

In January a stalk emerges from the heart of the foliage, bearing at its summit a cluster of fragrant dusky orange flowers. Each bloom, and there may be fifteen, is trumpet-shaped and beautiful.

LOCATION: Good light, but protect from hot sun. An east window is ideal. Give ample room.

HEIGHT: Tall—to 2 feet.

SOIL: Rich garden loam with some humus and manure added.

WATERING: Let soil dry between waterings. When the plant is growing and budding, keep moist.

FRAGRANCE: Fresh, subtle, and spicy.

SPECIAL CARE: Benefits from a summer out of doors in partial shade. Rest in a cool window (about 55° F.) until Christmas. Then bring to warmth and sun. Water more abundantly and feed weekly. Repot every three to five years, and at that time incorporate a few handfuls of manure in the soil.

►

LIME, PERSIAN (*Citrus aurantifolia*)

Another handsome citrus for the window garden, and one whose pure-white flowers diffuse their aroma all through the house. Limes *will* form on this bush, similar to the commercial variety. When they ripen, they enhance the plant for weeks. Requirements are the same as those for the American wonder lemon.

▼

LIVING VASE PLANT (*Aechmea* 'Foster's Favorite')

A nearly indestructible bromeliad from South America with striking foliage and exotic blooms. Called living vase plant because of the hollow cuplike center surrounded by a rosette of lacquered, lance-shaped, wine-red leaves. Give the plant sun to maintain leaf color and permit the remarkable deep blue flowers to develop.

LOCATION: Filtered sun. An east window is ideal.

HEIGHT: To 2 feet, but flowers when a little over 1 foot.

SOIL: A mixture of sand, leaf mold, peat moss, chopped osmunda fiber and rich earth.

WATERING: Soak thoroughly and permit to dry before rewatering. Keep the "vase" filled. Spray foliage frequently.

PROPAGATION: Young plants develop at the base of the foliage. Pot these separately with some root attached to each.

SPECIAL CARE: Never spray with insecticides. If scale develops, scrub off with soap and water.

▼

MYRTLE (*Myrtus communis microphylla*)

The classic myrtle of ancient Greece. Each compact little bush is covered with tiny dark-green aromatic leaves. The plant is starred with deeply scented white flowers in summer and fall. When blossoms fade, blue berries take their place, and last well into the winter. Prune as you would a privet hedge to keep neat and shapely.

LOCATION: Filtered sun or bright sun. ▶ Temperature preferred 55° F. to 60° F.

HEIGHT: 1 to 2 feet.

SOIL: Ordinary garden earth.

WATERING: Permit to dry between waterings.

FRAGRANCE: Both blossoms and foliage are aromatic.

PROPAGATION: Four- to six-inch cuttings taken in the spring will readily root in garden soil.

## MARGUERITE, BLUE (*Felicia amelloides*)

Native to South Africa. Delightful blue daisies literally hide the foliage of this cheerful plant that flowers continuously all winter. Do not try to hold it over for a second season, but make cuttings, or purchase a new plant.

LOCATION: Full sun. Preferred temperature in the 60's.

HEIGHT: Medium—to 15 inches.

SOIL: Regular earth from the garden.

WATERING: Soak thoroughly, let dry, and then rewater. Set the pot up to the rim in a bowl of water weekly to be sure the long deep roots get their share of moisture.

PROPAGATION: Six-inch stem cuttings taken in the spring will root in average soil. Pot individually and keep in semi-shade in the window, or the garden. Water frequently. By autumn new plants will be ready for a winter of bloom. ▶

## MOSES–IN–A–BOAT, MOSES–IN–THE–CRADLE, MOSES–ON–A–RAFT (*Rhoeo spathacea*)

From the West Indies and Mexico comes this remarkable plant, an easy variety to raise. Deep-green glossy leaves with pointed tips and bright purple undersides grow in a flaring rosette. White flowers appear from two purple boat-shaped bracts.

LOCATION: Full sun, also east or west window. Ordinary house temperature suits well.

HEIGHT: Medium—to 1 foot.

SOIL: Ordinary garden loam.

WATERING: More than average—should be kept damp but never soggy.

PROPAGATION: Annually sends up small clusters of new plantlets around the base, especially after a summer in the garden. These may be gently separated and potted individually.

79

## NERVE PLANT (*Fittonia argyroneura*) ▶

From Persia comes this ideal plant for wherever you have high humidity, perhaps your kitchen or a bathroom. The oval leaves with rounded ends are beautifully traced with delicate white veins. Flourishes in a terrarium where the air is always moist.

LOCATION: Filtered sunlight, east or west window.

HEIGHT: Low-growing. Trails over the pot rim.

SOIL: Garden loam with peat moss and humus added, and a little leaf mold if you have it.

WATERING: More than average. Keep damp but never sodden. Spray the foliage at least once a day.

PROPAGATION: Four-inch stem cuttings root readily in moist sand or soil. Bury the ends one or two inches in the medium used.

## NORFOLK ISLAND PINE (*Araucaria* ▶ *excelsa*)

A miniature evergreen which grows to 200 feet in its native habitat! Tiers of symmetrically arranged branches appear at regular intervals up a central stalk. Each set, usually of six, represents a year's growth. The bright green furry needles are soft and pleasant to touch. If kept pot-bound, the seedlings sold for indoor growing will not attain too formidable a height.

LOCATION: East or west window, even north. Filtered sunlight preferred. Ideal temperature 50° F. to 60° F.

HEIGHT: About 1 to 3 feet.

SOIL: Ordinary garden loam.

WATERING: Soil should be allowed to remain dry a day between thorough waterings.

SPECIAL CARE: Should be repotted only when the container becomes crammed with roots. This may be every two or three years.

OLEANDER (*Nerium oleander*)

Rare but easy-to-grow plant native to the shores of the Mediterranean and Asia Minor. In early spring clusters of blossoms, pink, red, yellow, or white, appear among the slender creamy yellow-edged leaves. Oleander blooms when very small and grows fast. To keep within bounds, annually trim back one-quarter of the plant. After the flowering period, rest with less sun and less water.

LOCATION: Full sun, south exposure. Must have plenty of room. Not for a small apartment. Grows best in a conservatory or small greenhouse in winter, on a sunny terrace or porch in summer.

HEIGHT: Flowering best when 5 feet or more.

SOIL: Rich garden loam with a trowelful of decomposed manure in the container.

WATERING: More than average. Water copiously when in bud and flower.

PROPAGATION: Six-inch cuttings root easily in moist sand or soil.

ORCHID (*Cattleya* varieties)

Certain orchids will thrive in a cool indoor garden or bay window. Buy plants in bud and you are sure of flowers in a few weeks. Pause when you can and study the detail in each bloom.

LOCATION: Filtered sun, an east or west window. Ideal temperature 55° F. by night and 65° F. by day, with high humidity.

HEIGHT: Medium—to 20 inches.

SOIL: Most orchids must be potted in osmunda fiber, chopped fir bark, or another special orchid-rooting medium.

WATERING: Tops should be sprayed daily or oftener with warm water. Roots should dry thoroughly between soakings. Foliage needs sponging several times a week, both leaves and pseudo-bulbs.

FRAGRANCE: Blossoms of many cattleyas are deeply fragrant.

ORANGE, OTAHEITE (*Citrus taitensis*)

Pink-tinged flowers appear among the foliage and remain open for weeks. Golden-orange fruits follow, plum-sized and with a limelike flavor. Blooms and fruits are on the branches at the same time and often when the plant is less than a foot tall. The fruits remain bright and colorful for weeks.

LOCATION: Full sun, south window.

HEIGHT: 1 to 3 feet.

SOIL: Rich garden loam with humus and manure added.

WATERING: Soak, and permit to dry before rewatering.

FRAGRANCE: Flowers are scented like the true orange blossoms.

SPECIAL CARE: To be sure of fruit, hand-pollinate. With a paintbrush dust the powdery pollen from one flower onto the stigma of another. Do this when the stigma is moist and sticky. Treat yellowing leaves with a little supplementary iron from a garden supply store.

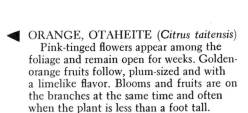

81

ORCHID (*Epidendrum radicans*)

Red or orange flowers come in rounded heads. Within each floret may be seen the Easter cross. Blossoms keep developing and the plant remains in flower for months, bringing a gay, exotic note to your window.

LOCATION. Filtered sun, full sun. Humidity needed. Ideal temperature 55° F. at night, 70° F. by day.

HEIGHT: Tall, to 2 feet, and slim.

SOIL: Plant in fir bark, osmunda fiber, or other orchid-rooting mediums.

WATERING: Soak thoroughly; let the roots remain dry a day or two before you drench again. Spray foliage daily.

FRAGRANCE: A delicate and subtle scent.

PROPAGATION: Aerial roots appear opposite leaves near the tips of tallest branches. When these roots are two or three inches long, cut off the stem just below them with a sharp knife and pot in a separate container, roots folded in the osmunda.

SPECIAL CARE: Every two or three weeks wash off thick leaves with a soft brush and soapy water.

ORCHID (*Oncidium triquetrum*)

A small orchid with leaves, 2 or 3 inches tall, arranged in a casual fan shape. If conditions are suitable, individual scarlet flowers last on the plant in a fresh and pristine state for weeks, and more continue to develop during the winter and spring months.

LOCATION: Filtered sun, east or west window, south window if partially shaded. Humidity is a must. Will thrive in kitchen or bathroom.

HEIGHT: Low—to 6 inches.

SOIL: Osmunda fiber, chopped fir bark, or another special orchid medium.

WATERING: Soil should be allowed to remain dry a day or two between soakings. Foliage needs spraying several times a day.

ORCHID (*Paphiopedilum* 'Olivia')

This greenhouse lady's-slipper resembles its relatives, the pink, yellow, and white lady's-slipper orchids that grow wild in the spring woods. One of the terrestrial orchids, it is easy to grow if you supply cool nights and humid conditions. It often blooms twice a year, and the long-lasting flowers may need individual stakes for support.

LOCATION: Partial sun, east or west exposure, sunlight filtered through a 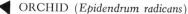 curtain or other plants.

HEIGHT: Small to medium; doesn't take up too much room vertically or horizontally.

SOIL: A rich, light earth with excellent drainage.

WATERING: Should be kept evenly moist at all times but never soggy. Needs daily spraying in bright weather.

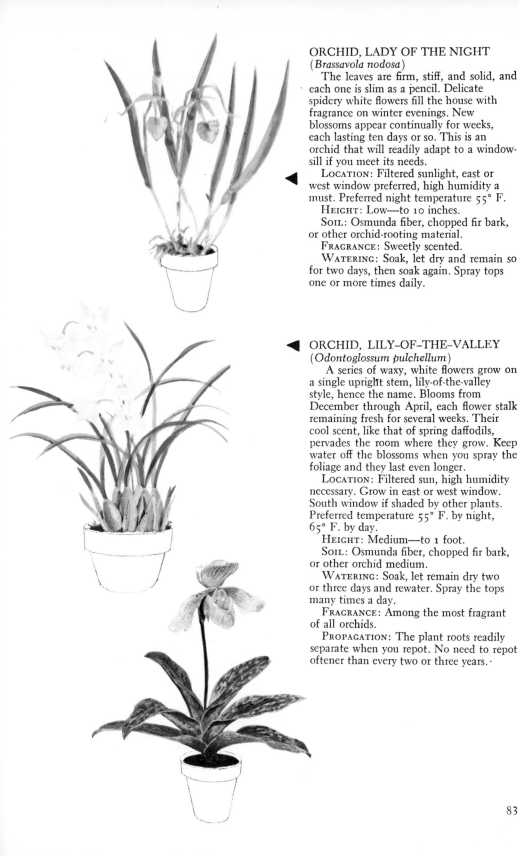

## ORCHID, LADY OF THE NIGHT
(*Brassavola nodosa*)

The leaves are firm, stiff, and solid, and each one is slim as a pencil. Delicate spidery white flowers fill the house with fragrance on winter evenings. New blossoms appear continually for weeks, each lasting ten days or so. This is an orchid that will readily adapt to a window-sill if you meet its needs.

LOCATION: Filtered sunlight, east or west window preferred, high humidity a must. Preferred night temperature 55° F.

HEIGHT: Low—to 10 inches.

SOIL: Osmunda fiber, chopped fir bark, or other orchid-rooting material.

FRAGRANCE: Sweetly scented.

WATERING: Soak, let dry and remain so for two days, then soak again. Spray tops one or more times daily.

## ORCHID, LILY–OF–THE–VALLEY
(*Odontoglossum pulchellum*)

A series of waxy, white flowers grow on a single upright stem, lily-of-the-valley style, hence the name. Blooms from December through April, each flower stalk remaining fresh for several weeks. Their cool scent, like that of spring daffodils, pervades the room where they grow. Keep water off the blossoms when you spray the foliage and they last even longer.

LOCATION: Filtered sun, high humidity necessary. Grow in east or west window. South window if shaded by other plants. Preferred temperature 55° F. by night, 65° F. by day.

HEIGHT: Medium—to 1 foot.

SOIL: Osmunda fiber, chopped fir bark, or other orchid medium.

WATERING: Soak, let remain dry two or three days and rewater. Spray the tops many times a day.

FRAGRANCE: Among the most fragrant of all orchids.

PROPAGATION: The plant roots readily separate when you repot. No need to repot oftener than every two or three years. ·

83

OXALIS (*Oxalis martiana 'Aurea-reticu-lata'*) ▶

A compact little plant with bright-green clover-like leaves. Five-petaled flowers, rosy-red, pink, yellow, and white, nod cheerily all winter and spring.

LOCATION: Full sun, southern exposure preferred. Ideal temperature about 60° F.

HEIGHT: Low and small; doesn't take up too much room vertically or horizontally.

WATERING: Keep evenly moist while in bloom, gradually decreasing water as leaves wither. Store dry while dormant.

SOIL: Plant in rich soil with leaf mold and humus incorporated. Provide excellent drainage.

SPECIAL CARE: Oxalis needs a period of complete rest after flowering, with less light and no water. Repot in fresh earth in the fall, bring to a sunny window and start watering again.

OXALIS (*Oxalis ortgiesii*)

A branching upright plant with interestingly marked trifoliate leaves, deep-green above, maroon beneath. The red-stemmed yellow flowers grow in clusters and bloom almost continuously.

◀ LOCATION: Full sun. Thrives in a warm room.

HEIGHT: Low—to 8 inches.

SOIL: Regular garden earth.

WATERING: Should be watered sparingly except when the plant is producing new leaves, buds, and flowers.

SPECIAL CARE: After the flowers stop blooming, water should be withheld. The leaves soon wither and drop. In late summer plant should be repotted in fresh earth, brought to the sunny window, and watering begun again.

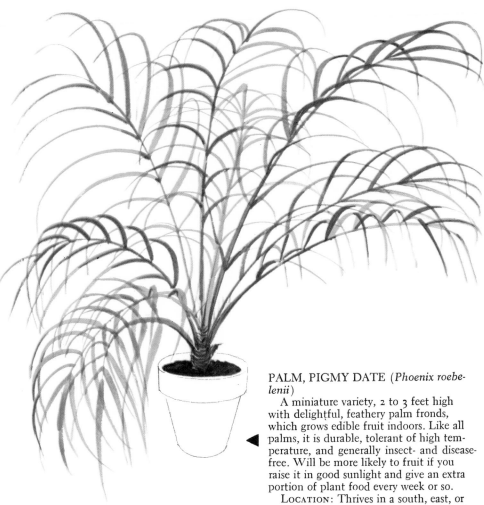

**PALM, PIGMY DATE** (*Phoenix roebelenii*)

A miniature variety, 2 to 3 feet high with delightful, feathery palm fronds, which grows edible fruit indoors. Like all palms, it is durable, tolerant of high temperature, and generally insect- and disease-free. Will be more likely to fruit if you raise it in good sunlight and give an extra portion of plant food every week or so.

LOCATION: Thrives in a south, east, or west window, and even an interior location will suit if it receives good light.

SOIL: Rich garden loam with leaf mold, humus, and decomposed manure added. Good drainage essential.

HEIGHT: 2 to 3 feet.

WATERING: Keep evenly moist but never soggy throughout the summer, somewhat drier in winter. Sponge leaves occasionally to keep them clean and to satisfy the plant's humidity needs.

**OXALIS** (*Oxalis variabilis*)

A native of the Andes and South Africa with clover-shaped leaves. Bright rose, white, or violet five-petaled flowers open almost all winter. Blossoms and leaves fold up at night. The plant stem curves gracefully out of the pot to trail over the windowsill; the blooms also spill down in a tumbling cascade, making this a fine subject for a hanging basket.

LOCATION: Filtered sun, east or west window.

HEIGHT: Trails and spreads. Needs ample space horizontally.

SOIL: Rich garden loam with humus added.

WATERING: Average. Soil should be allowed to dry between soakings.

▲

## PANDA PLANT (*Kalanchoe tomentosa*)

A succulent from Madagascar whose thick, inflexible leaves, light gray-green, are covered with "fur." They have the appearance of soft wool, and brown "stitches" decorate their rims. The foliage is so velvety you want to touch it. A window garden plant to grow for texture, for the pleasure of handling as well as the looking.

LOCATION: Sun, and more sun in fall and winter. At other times a semishady window is preferred.

HEIGHT: Medium—to 15 inches.

SOIL: Equal parts loam, leaf mold, sand, and humus, and a little gravel. Good drainage is important.

WATERING: During fall and winter, the growing and flowering time, soak, let dry thoroughly and then rewater. Rest after blooming, watering lightly about once a week.

PROPAGATION: Very easy. In spring or summer break off a stem or even a leaf. Place in a shaded, airy spot until the cut end is completely dry. Set a half-inch deep in sand, place in filtered sun, water sparingly. When the leaf plumps up and becomes green again, it has taken hold. When new growth appears, bring to a sunny window and give more water.

▲

## PATIENCE, PATIENT LUCY (*Impatiens sultanii*)

An old-fashioned favorite. Its popular name of patience is a rather surprising reversal of its Latin name. The idea the Latin name means to convey is "don't touch"—the fruits "explode" on touch after maturity. The fleshy foliage grows rapidly, and red, pink, coral or white flowers open the year round.

LOCATION: Full sun, south window.

HEIGHT: Medium to tall. May be pruned drastically. Its charm is doubled when the shape is symmetrical and compact.

SOIL: Rich garden loam.

WATERING: More than average. Should be kept moist except once about every ten days, when it should dry out thoroughly before being rewatered.

PROPAGATION: Easy. Every six-inch stem that is pruned off may be set in sand or earth. It should be watered sparingly lest it rot before new growth starts.

**PERUVIAN DAFFODIL** (*Hymenocallis* ▶
*calathina*)

Great white flowers like lilacs with
shredded petal tips. As with the amaryllis,
pot in a container only one inch larger
than the bulb, and with the top half of
the bulb above the soil. It takes eight
weeks from planting to bloom. Until first
signs of life appear, don't water at all.
The first growth is a flower bud; leaves
follow.

LOCATION: Filtered sun—an eastern or
western exposure.

HEIGHT: Medium—to 15 inches.

SOIL: Rich garden loam with humus
and a handful of dried manure added.

WATERING: Give ample food and water
after growth commences.

FRAGRANCE: A delightful scent somewhat like that of the orange blossom.

SPECIAL CARE: To be sure of next
year's bloom, fertilize after the flowers
fold and drop. Continue watering until
June, then set container and all in the
garden. In autumn let dry off until leaves
fall; replace the top inch of old soil with
new.

**PHILODENDRON** (*Philodendron* × ▶
*Mandianum*)

A slow climber whose uncurling new
growth is a magnificent red. A young leaf
first appears slim as a pencil. Gradually
it unrolls into a pleasing heart-shaped leaf.
After the fifth leaf has developed, place a
pole, or piece of bark, in the pot as a
support.

LOCATION: Full sun, filtered sun, no
sun. An adaptable plant.

HEIGHT: Climbs. May be pruned to any
height desired.

SOIL: Regular garden loam.

WATERING: More than average. Water
thoroughly, let dry, and immediately
water again.

PROPAGATION: A leaf with a long stem
placed in a separate pot with the bottom
of the stem two inches under the soil will
soon become an independent plant.

◀ **PEPEROMIA, WATERMELON
BEGONIA** (*Peperomia sandersii argyreia*)

A South American tropical plant related
to neither a watermelon nor a begonia
but instead to the genus which yields
common black pepper. Red leaf stems and
silver-striped foliage give this little plant
a gay look and sometimes suggest the
markings on a watermelon.

LOCATION: East or west exposure, or
sunlight filtered through a curtain in a
south window. Even thrives in a north
window with plenty of light. Likes warmth
and high humidity.

HEIGHT: Low.

SOIL: Ordinary garden loam with humus
added.

WATERING: More than average. Soil
should be allowed to approach dryness
between soakings. Foliage should be
sprayed daily or oftener.

PROPAGATION: A leaf with an inch or so
of stem will root rapidly in damp sand or
soil. The stem should be placed completely
under the rooting medium, and the pot
covered with an upturned tumbler or
plastic bag. It should be aired briefly once
a day.

87

## PHILODENDRON, WINDOWLEAF
### (*Monstera deliciosa*)

Firm leaves—cut, slashed, shiny and with definite veins—decorate this astonishing grower, known to florists as *Philodendron pertusum*, a juvenile leaf form of *Monstera deliciosa*. It is native to Brazil and to all tropics and rain forests. Here, next to orchids, it settles in lower branches of trees, flourishing among ferns and mosses. In spite of its tropical origin, it thrives indoors in our northern climate and grows rampantly. Prune both roots

and top drastically.

LOCATION: Full sun, filtered sun, no sun.

HEIGHT: Climbs to your ceiling if you don't limit it.

SOIL: Ordinary garden loam.

WATERING: Average. Water thoroughly, let it remain dry a day or two, then soak again. Spray the foliage daily, sponge off every week or so.

PROPAGATION: A leaf set in a separate pot, with the stem a few inches under the soil, will soon become a new plant.

## PHILODENDRON (*Philodendron oxycardium*)

The common philodendron of the ten-cent stores. Foolproof, reliable, and easiest of all vines. Grows even in dim light. In one short season it becomes a veritable tangle. Philodendron will even flourish in a room where cooking gas is used, and this causes most plants to rebel. The shiny red-pointed buds uncurl into appealing heart-shaped leaves. This hardy vine thrives in water for weeks but not too well indefinitely. Give it support and it climbs, or let it trail; and keep the branch ends trimmed for a compact plant.

LOCATION: Filtered sun, no sun, full sun. An interior location. Just about anywhere.

HEIGHT: Climbs and trails.

SOIL: Ordinary garden loam.

WATERING: Soak; let dry thoroughly before rewatering. Do not drown the plant with overwatering or the leaves turn yellow and fall.

PROPAGATION: Any stem three to six inches long will root in a few weeks in water or soil and become a flourishing new plant in two months or so.

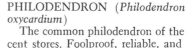

▲

## PILEA (*Pilea involucrata*)

Glossy, dark-green, flat leaves with interesting lighter veins. The miniature flowers grow in clusters and appear to be stemless and resting on the leaves themselves. When small, the pilea makes a fine terrarium subject.

LOCATION: Filtered sun, east or west window.

HEIGHT: Low—to 6 inches; spreads. Give elbow room.

SOIL: Rich garden loam with a little decomposed manure added.

WATERING: More than average. Keep moist most of the time, but every ten days or so, let pot soil become thoroughly dry before rewatering.

PROPAGATION: Break off a leaf-tipped branch, and root in a new pot of soil, burying the end an inch or two beneath the earth.

▲

## PIGGYBACK PLANT, MOTHER–OF–THOUSANDS (*Tolmiea menziesii*)

In its native woodlands of the Pacific Northwest, strange green flowers develop on this plant. But they rarely bloom indoors. We raise the plant for its foliage of broad, attractive, many-pointed leaves covered with delicate fuzz. The light-green leaflets are carried piggyback on the old leaves. If you don't prune the new leaflets, they may reach a neighboring pot, take root and start a new young plant.

LOCATION: Filtered sun, and even better, no sun. A north window with good light is ideal. Preferred temperature 65° F. But this is an adaptable plant.

HEIGHT: Low—to 6 inches.

SOIL: Regular garden loam with compost added.

WATERING: Average. Soak, let dry thoroughly before rewatering.

PROPAGATION: Plant stem of parent leaf bearing the tiny cluster of new leaflets up to its base in ordinary soil. Within a few weeks fresh growth tells you that the plant has taken hold.

◄ PINEAPPLE SAGE (*Salvia rutilans*)

Flowers in tones of scarlet appear through the fall and winter. If the temperature is too warm and dry, the blossoms are small, few, and scattered. For best results, settle it in a cool part of the window garden or on a sun porch.

LOCATION: Preferred temperature 60° F. but requires full sun. A south window in a cool room with high humidity is ideal.

HEIGHT: Medium—to 15 inches.

SOIL: Ordinary garden loam with a little compost added.

WATERING: More than average. Keep moist but never soggy. Once every two weeks let dry between waterings.

FRAGRANCE: Leaves pungent and pineapple-scented.

89

◄ POINSETTIA (*Euphorbia pulcherrima*)

The monarch of the holiday season was named for Joel A. Poinsett, from South Carolina, who, in 1828, first saw the plant in Mexico. He sent some cuttings home for propagation. It is the blossom bracts of the poinsettia that are bright red, pink, or white. Golden cups in the center of these colored bracts are the flowers.

LOCATION: Full sun. Preferred temperature 60° F. by night, 65° F. by day.

HEIGHT: To 3 feet. Grows to 5 or 6 feet in the South and in California.

SOIL: Rich garden loam with humus added.

WATERING: Average. Soil should be allowed to dry thoroughly between soakings.

PROPAGATION: Cuttings of ten-inch sections of stem are made in the spring. These should be set in separate containers. in the garden with the end of each two to four inches under the pot soil. In filtered sunlight they will readily root and become new plants.

◄ PRIMROSE (*Primula malacoides*)

Sky-blue, rose, red, magenta, purple, or white flat clusters of bloom top 6-inch stems that rise from the heart of the plant in never-ending succession all season, in fact, often for a whole year. However, don't try to hold the plant over for a second winter. It uses most of its vigor in that first year of prolific bloom.

LOCATION: A cool part of the window garden in partial sun. East or west exposure ideal. A south window if shaded by other plants. Preferred night temperature 65° F.

HEIGHT: Medium—to 12 inches.

SOIL: Ordinary garden loam. Plant with the crown a little above the soil surface so water runs toward the pot rim and does not settle in the plant center and cause it to rot.

WATERING: Very important to keep earth constantly moist, and *never* let the roots dry out.

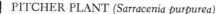

PITCHER PLANT *(Sarracenia purpurea)*

Native to swamps and savannas from Virginia and Alabama to Newfoundland. A bizarre and sinister plant that snares flies and spiders and dines on them. The leaf, a hollow red-veined trumpet filled with fluid, is, in reality, a cleverly arranged trap. The insect is lured deep into the recesses by downward-pointing hairs that make the going practically one-way. When he finally slips to the bottom, he drowns in the liquid collected there and is eventually digested by the plant. The flower petals are bright yellow and the umbrella-like stigma-style area turns vivid red.

LOCATION: Filtered sun. East or west window, or shaded south window.

HEIGHT: Medium—to 10 inches.

SOIL: Sphagnum, sand, and leaf mold mixed and moistened to a mucky, boggy consistency.

WATERING: Should be kept constantly damp but never with alkaline water. Rain water is the safest, and surest.

PRAYER PLANT *(Maranta leuconeura 'Kerchoveana')*

Light-green, velvety leaves have interesting markings that turn from green to chocolate-purple as the foliage ages. The flowers are insignificant but it is the prayer part that is intriguing. At dusk the leaves which have been at right angles to their stems all day move up slowly like arms reaching high in supplication. At dawn they bend back to their horizontal positions.

LOCATION: Partial shade, east or west window. Will also grow in a northern exposure. Never wants a strong sun beating on it. Keep night temperature at least up to 65° F. and give high humidity. Thrives in kitchen and bathroom.

HEIGHT: Low—to 8 inches.

SOIL: Rich earth with good drainage.

WATERING: Syringe foliage daily and keep pot soil moist. In autumn when plant rests, water less frequently.

SPECIAL CARE: Every fall trim off the oldest leaves or any that look straggly.

RESURRECTION PLANT *(Selaginella lepidophylla)*

A ball of tangled, dried-up fronds revives after a short time in water and unfolds into a healthy, rich-green, fully alive plant. Keeps for years in the dry state, if you want to take it out of water and let it dry out.

LOCATION: Filtered sun, full sun. South, east, or west exposure.

HEIGHT: Low—to 6 inches.

SOIL: Ordinary garden loam after the plant has been completely revived in water.

WATERING: Keep moist at all times.

91

**RUBBER PLANT** (*Ficus elastica*)

This most rugged of house plants comes from Malaya. It will grow, quite neglected, in a dark corner. However, with light and sun the leaves develop a fine heavy texture. Sponge off the foliage about every two weeks with soap and warm water to keep it clean and glossy. Observe how the young leaves unwind, contrasting their fresh new green with the darker, older foliage. No special soil, location, or care required.

LOCATION: Adapts to any spot. Partial sun preferred.

HEIGHT: Tall—to 4 feet. Prune to fit your space.

SOIL: Ordinary garden loam.

WATERING: Let dry thoroughly between waterings. Occasionally set pot in a pail of water so that the deep-reaching roots receive their full share of moisture.

SPECIAL CARE: Oiling or artificially shining the foliage of the rubber plant, or other foliage plants with large leaves, fills in the pores and prevents the leaves from breathing.

▼

▲

**ROSE, MINIATURE** (*Rosa chinensis* var. *minima*)

Discovered by the late Dr. Roulet, blooming in the window of a chalet in Switzerland where it had been popular for centuries. Sometimes incorrectly known as *Rosa rouletti*. Tiny, shell-pink blossoms develop on a 4-inch-high plant and continue blooming for weeks at a time. Avoid exposure to cooking gas. Benefits from a summer in the garden in full sun.

LOCATION: South window. High humidity is vital to the success of miniature roses indoors.

HEIGHT: Low—to 6 inches.

SOIL: Rich garden loam with decomposed manure and humus added. Give ample root room. A five-inch pot is the best size.

WATERING: Plenty of moisture at the roots constantly. These flourish in wick-fed pots. Spray the foliage many times a day or grow under glass. See below.

FRAGRANCE: Most sorts are fragrant with that familiar fresh, sweet, rose scent.

SPECIAL CARE: Raising roses in the house is a particular challenge. Here are some useful hints: Grow them under glass either in a terrarium, or under a bell jar or a large glass tumbler. Moisture is vital but they also need a daily airing. To coax into a long flowering season, don't water too much in November or December and keep relatively cool. In January bring to warmth, more water, and all the sun there is.

## SEA GRAPE (*Coccoloba uvifera*)

An American tropical tree that grows to 20 feet in its native habitat, but will be considerably more restrained in a pot indoors. The attractive, shiny, green foliage has light veining and a red rib on each leaf. The leaves flare, fold, and curve, and each one has a rather casual, ruffled appearance. The sea grape proves a dramatic accent in a sunny living room where it soon becomes a small bush. Sponge the leaves off with soap and water every few weeks.

LOCATION: Full sun; give ample space.
HEIGHT: Tall—to 6 or 8 feet.
SOIL: Ordinary garden loam.
WATERING: Keep moist but never soggy.

▼

## ROSEMARY (*Rosmarinus officinalis*)

Rosemary is from the Latin meaning "sea dew" and was so named because it is found wild on the sea cliffs of Southern France. Crush a few needles between your fingers to release that wonderful aroma. Legend tells us that the Virgin washed her sky-blue cloak and spread it to dry over a rosemary bush and the flowers were henceforth blue. Ever since, rosemary is reputed to bring luck.

LOCATION: Does best in a cool part of the window garden, but must have full sun. Ideal temperature 60° F., no higher.
HEIGHT: Medium—to 15 inches.
SOIL: Ordinary garden loam.
WATERING: Whenever the soil feels dry, water.
FRAGRANCE: Deeply scented foliage, combining fragrances of nutmeg, wisteria and pine needles.

▼

## SEA ONION (*Ornithogalum caudatum*)

An easy and rewarding house plant. Observe the green streamers emerging from the top of the bulb. Cut them short; they curl into ringlets. Let them grow long, and they trail down two or three feet. Blossoms form on a long curving stalk and consist of a whole sheath of white starry flowers, each one delicate as a snowflake and with an intricately formed green center.

LOCATION: Full sun, south window; partial sun, east or west window. Hardy, adapts to all exposures.

HEIGHT: Medium—to 15 inches.

SOIL: Average garden loam with a little sand and humus added. Set the top half of the bulb above the soil.

WATERING: Soak, let dry thoroughly, then rewater.

PROPAGATION: Plant continually sheds a series of skins. Beneath each layer lies a group of small bulblets, each one a shiny peppermint green. As these ripen, they fall from the parent plant and may be potted, a dozen or more in one container. Set every bulblet an inch under the soil. When it sends up a few streamers and grows to cherry size, move to a pot of its own and plant it partly out of the soil.

SPECIAL CARE: In too hot and dry an atmosphere, the foliage may develop a kind of scale. To control and eliminate this, scrub the leaves with soapy water and a soft brush. ▼

## SEERSUCKER PLANT (*Geogenanthus undatus*)

An unusual tropical plant from Peru. The smooth-edged leaves are rich purple beneath and striped silver on the top. They also have a puckered "seersucker" texture that suggests the familiar fabric. Dense clusters of blue flowers appear annually.

LOCATION: Filtered sun, east or west window.

HEIGHT: Low to medium. Usually about 1 foot.

SOIL: Rich garden loam.

WATERING: Soil should be kept moist but never soggy. Foliage needs frequent spraying to remind it of its native tropical habitat.

▼

## SHRIMP PLANT (*Beloperone guttata*)

From Mexico and Brazil come this rewarding indoor plant. White flowers emerge from delicate, trailing, shrimp-pink bracts and these remain on the plant from November to April. Never hesitate to shape and to trim drastically, lest it grow out of hand. Benefits from a summer in the garden loose in the soil. Prune radically before you repot in September, and bring in the house.

LOCATION: Adapts to a sunny south exposure, also to an east or west one. Grow in a warm part of the window garden and a warm room.

HEIGHT: Medium to tall. About 20 inches, but flowers when only 10 inches high.

SOIL: Rich garden loam with extra humus added.

WATERING: Soak, allow to become almost dry, and then rewater.

▼

## SENSITIVE PLANT (*Mimosa pudica*)

Tramping through sweeps of this plant on the remote volcano slopes of Guatemala, and watching the leaves temporarily wither in your wake, gives you an eerie sensation. Indoors, its amazing foliage wilts at the touch of the human hand but left alone soon perks up again. Plenty of sun and water keep it flourishing a long season in the house. Each bloom, the size and shape of a cherry, is like a lavender pincushion stuck full of white pins. These appear annually and last weeks.

LOCATION: Full sun, south window. Warm room with high humidity.

HEIGHT: Medium—to 15 inches.

SOIL: Ordinary garden loam.

WATERING: Soil should be kept moist, never allowed to dry out. Foliage should be sprayed daily or oftener to increase humidity.

▼

## SIDERASIS (*Siderasis fuscata*)

Oval green leaves, with purple undersides and a white midrib, grow in a clustering rosette. Note the velvety red hairs on both sides of young and mature leaves. Lavender-blue blossoms touched with white appear in the heart of the plant, usually in late winter and spring.

LOCATION: Filtered sun, no sun. With excellent light, flourishes in an interior location. Ideal temperature 70° F. day and night.

HEIGHT: Low—to 6 inches.

SOIL: Average garden loam with a handful of decomposed manure added.

WATERING: Soak, let dry thoroughly, then rewater.

PROPAGATION: Pot new plantlets that develop at the base of the parent plant.

## SILK OAK, AUSTRALIAN (*Grevillea robusta*)

A 100-foot flowering tree—in the tropics. But grown in the house, it becomes a delightful foliage plant and remains an appropriate size. Curving branches develop, with clusters of lacy leaves. If you have space, plant the silk oak in a tub and let it grow to a small indoor tree.

LOCATION: Filtered sun in an east, west or south window. Ideal temperature 50° F. to 60° F., but it will grow in a warmer temperature.

HEIGHT: 2 to 10 feet.

SOIL: Rich garden loam.

WATERING: Keep moist but not soaking-wet. Mist-spray the leaves daily.

PROPAGATION: Seed, obtainable from house-plant nurseries, will grow into a good-sized plant within a year.

## SNAILFLOWER; CORKSCREW FLOWER (*Phaseolus caracalla*)

An unusual tropical plant seldom seen, but one that merits more attention. Easy to raise in the house. Clusters of lavender flowers emerge from spiral buds which suggest the twist of a snail shell.

LOCATION: Warm room, full sun, south, east, or west window. High humidity needed.

HEIGHT: Trails, spreads, climbs.

SOIL: Ordinary garden loam with a little humus added.

WATERING: More than average. Soil should be kept moist almost all the time, but never sodden. Foliage needs spraying many times a day.

## SNAKE PLANT (*Sansevieria trifasciata*)

This import from South Africa is so hardy it will thrive anywhere even when badly neglected. However, if properly cared for, it produces charming flowers. A tall blossom spike rises from the heart of the plant. Buds, like beads on a necklace, spread along the stalk and open into fragrant green-white or pale-yellow blooms.

LOCATION: Will adapt to any exposure —north, south, east, west, or an interior location. Must have sun to bloom, however.

HEIGHT: Medium to tall—and slim.

SOIL: Gritty, sandy, gravelly earth with humus added.

WATERING: Soil should be kept dry for a week between thorough waterings. Leaves should be sponged off occasionally with clear water.

FRAGRANCE: Sweet-scented blossoms.

PROPAGATION: A leaf may be cut into three-inch pieces and each one set upright and one-inch deep in sand or soil. A new plant connected by an underground stem appears at a little distance from the section of leaf planted.

 SPATHE FLOWER (*Spathiphyllum cannaefolium*)

This eye-catching flower, like a cross between a jack-in-the-pulpit and a calla lily, thrives in the window garden. Light-green, lance-shaped leaves with deep center ribs twist and bend in an attractive manner. It blooms prolifically all winter. A pale-green outer sheath turns white and opens to reveal a spike of miniature snowy blossoms within.

LOCATION: Filtered sun, east or west window. Also no sun will suit its fancy, but it must have good light. Preferred temperature 65° F. to 70° F. Needs high humidity.

SOIL: Half garden loam, half humus. Should be repotted each fall.

WATERING: Soil needs daily watering. Foliage should be mist-sprayed one or more times each day and sponged off once a week to remove house dust.

FRAGRANCE: Flowers deeply scented.

SPIRAL GINGER; SPIRAL FLAG (*Costus igneus*)

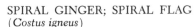

A rare but easy house plant from Brazil. In the spring it bears three-inch flowers with rugged petals of brilliant orange. Attractive, smooth, slim, glossy leaves are arranged spirally on the stalks.

LOCATION: Filtered sun, east or west window. Warm room with preferred temperature 65° F. to 75° F. High humidity needed.

HEIGHT: Tall—to 3 feet. Needs ample space in all directions.

SOIL: Regular garden loam.

WATERING: More than average. Roots should be kept moist but never soggy. Foliage should be sprayed once a day or oftener.

## STAR–OF–BETHLEHEM, ITALIAN ▶
BELLFLOWER (*Campanula isophylla*)

A free-blooming plant from Italy. Beginning in July and continuing until November, starry white flowers shower in great profusion over the casual trailing foliage. Shape it to keep compact and trim. After the flowers fade, prune back drastically, thin out old stems to give new ones room to grow. Rest for eight weeks or so, watering less, then repot in fresh soil, feed, and bring back to the sunny window.

LOCATION: A cool south window. In summer, filtered sun.

HEIGHT: Trails. Grow in a hanging basket or regular pot.

SOIL: Rich garden loam with humus added.

WATERING: More than average. Keep moist when blooming but during the winter while resting let remain somewhat drier.

## STONE–AND–WINDOW PLANT,
PEBBLE PLANT (*Lithops* species)

◀ Meeting these South African desert plants for the first time, you might think someone had tossed a handful of pebbles over the top of a flowerpot of earth. The "leaves" suggest stones, and the semi-transparent tips are "windows." Through these, sunlight filters into the photosynthetic tissue that nourishes each leaf. Large, fragrant anemone-like flowers emerge annually, often in August. The plants grow thickly, and a stand of them in bloom is a veritable sheet of color.

LOCATION: Full sun, and the hotter and drier the better.

HEIGHT: Low—1 to 3 inches.

SOIL: Gritty, gravelly loam. Mostly sand with just a little peat moss added.

WATERING: In your window garden keep dry most of the time from November to May unless the plant seems to shrivel, then give a few drops of water. Water from May to November, but sparingly.

FRAGRANCE: Sweet-scented flowers.

## ◀ STRAWBERRY GERANIUM;
STRAWBERRY BEGONIA (*Saxifraga sarmentosa*)

Neither a geranium nor a begonia but a plant with a most appealing way of reproducing itself. Runners, similar to those on a true strawberry, emerge from the plant base. Each one terminates in a huddle of the tiniest leaves imaginable. These small plantlets dangle appealingly at the tips of the runners while reaching for new homes in neighboring pots. The mature leaves are bordered with pink scallops. The brighter the sunlight, the deeper the pinks.

LOCATION: Full sun, partial sun. Prefer a cool spot in the window.

HEIGHT: Low—to 4 inches.

SOIL: Ordinary garden loam with peat moss and leaf mold added. Grows best in a three- to four-inch pot.

WATERING: Soil should be kept moist but never soggy.

PROPAGATION: The new little leaf clusters may be anchored in the soil of another pot. When fresh growth appears, the runner should be cut to separate it from the parent.

99

◀ STREPTOCARPUS (*Streptocarpus saxorum*)

From South Africa comes a brand-new house plant, sometimes called Cape Primrose. The delicate four-petaled lavender flowers, whose buds are long, slim and horizontal, are in bloom for more than six months in succession, beginning in the fall. This rampant grower needs an annual repotting.

LOCATION: Full sun, east or west window also. Humid atmosphere needed. Preferred temperature 60° F. by night, 70° F. by day.

HEIGHT: Medium to 20 inches.

SOIL: A mixture of sand, humus, and garden loam.

WATERING: Keep constantly moist and spray the foliage many times a day.

STRING–OF–HEARTS VINE, ▶
ROSARY VINE (*Ceropegia woodii*)

Not a valentine, but a succulent from Natal, and an unusual vine for the window. The pleasing leaves are marbled white on green if grown in shade, white on copper if grown in full sun. In sun or shade the leaf's underside is an attractive rosy-gray. Violet urn-shaped flowers appear every summer.

LOCATION: No sun, or partial sun; north, east, or west window.

HEIGHT: Stems grow a yard or two and will trail or climb.

SOIL: Rich, sandy soil with humus added.

WATERING: Should be watered only when the soil feels dry to touch.

PROPAGATION: Six-inch stem cuttings root readily in sand or soil.

SPECIAL CARE: Occasionally the vine will take a brief rest. At this time leaves appear to wilt. It should be watered less until plant sends up new growth, then watered normally.

TEMPLE BELLS (*Smithiantha zebrina*) ▶

The green, plushy leaves of this Mexican import are amazingly patterned with purple veins. In midwinter at the top of the central stalk appears a spire of rich red flowers, each pendent floret flaring in a bell-like manner. New buds at the summit continue to open for weeks.

LOCATION: A warm room with high humidity. Filtered sun, east, west or south window.

HEIGHT: Low—to 10 inches.

SOIL: Rich loam, with humus and sand added.

WATERING: Keep moist while plant is producing new growth and is in bud and flower. At other times let dry between waterings. Spray foliage daily.

SPECIAL CARE: After the flowers pass, gradually withhold water until foliage dies down. Rest in a dark, cool place for three months or so, watering only every week to keep the roots from shriveling. When it begins to grow, bring back to the window and fertilize weekly.

SWEET OLIVE (*Osmanthus fragrans*)

Southeast Asia sent these small clusters of fragrant creamy flowers. The sweet olive has neat growing habits; it never grows leggy or becomes unwieldy, and never does an insect disturb it. Prune roots and top to keep it small and compact, or let it grow large if you have space. The smooth glossy olive-green leaves have a good firm feel. ◀ After a summer in the garden in a semi-shady spot the sweet olive rewards you with masses of flowers that begin to open in early autumn, and continue almost indefinitely.

LOCATION: Filtered sun or full sun. Thrives in an east, south, or west window.

HEIGHT: Medium—to 3 feet.

SOIL: Ordinary garden soil with humus, and leaf mold added.

WATERING: Keep soil slightly damp but never soggy.

FRAGRANCE: A rich fruity scent that fills the room, especially on sunny days after you have mist-sprayed.

SPECIAL CARE: Does best in a temperature in the 60's and can take 50° F. at night.

TILLANDSIA CYANEA

A bromeliad from the American tropics, easy to bring to flower in a partly sunny window. In the fall from a rosette of slim curling leaves a shocking-pink flower spike emerges and sends out a succession of navy-blue blossoms.

LOCATION: Filtered sunlight, east or west window.

HEIGHT: Medium—to 15 inches.

SOIL: Wrap the roots in osmunda and wire this plant to an eight-inch-square, one-inch-thick piece of cyprus wood. You may also grow it more conventionally in a pot.

WATERING: Let dry between soakings. Increase the water supply when it is actively growing or flowering; otherwise keep soil rather dry.

PROPAGATION: Offshoots that develop at the base of the plant may be cut apart with a sharp knife when a few inches high and potted individually.

▼

◀ UMBRELLA SEDGE (*Cyperus alternifolius*)

Native to the swamps of Africa. Graceful, ribbon-like streamers top each stalk and open out like casual umbrella spokes. Set the pot *in* a pebble tray of water. Here is a plant that actually benefits when the roots are *in water* and constantly moist.

LOCATION: Sun, filtered sun, or no sun with good light. In other words, most adaptable.

HEIGHT: Tall—to 3 feet, but may be kept to 20 inches or less by pruning.

SOIL: Rich garden loam.

WATERING: Keep water in saucer, but even better, set pot in pebble tray with the bottom constantly in water.

PROPAGATION: Roots readily separate for new plants any time of the year.

VELVET PLANT (*Gynura aurantiaca*)

A handsome plant from Java with leaves like rich, purple velvet. Both foliage and stems are covered with infinitesimal hairs, giving the whole plant a soft, plushy surface, wonderful to touch. The inconspicuous yellow or orange flowers are unimportant. We grow the velvet plant for its rich, royal color, and the foliage texture. The leaf color develops best in full sun and with moisture both at the roots and on the foliage.

LOCATION: Sun, south window. Preferred temperature 70° F. day and night.

HEIGHT: Low—to 10 inches.

SOIL: Average garden loam with humus and decomposed manure added.

WATERING: Roots should be kept moist and tops sprayed daily or oftener.

PROPAGATION: Six-inch stem cuttings from a mature plant will root in soil or sand. It is better to grow a new one than retain the parent. The old plant becomes straggly after two or three years.

▼

## UMBRELLA TREE, AUSTRALIAN ▶
(*Schefflera actinophylla*)

Attractive in four-inch pots, but also grows to a small tree if permitted. This attractive foliage plant has shiny leaflets grouped at the top of the stems. Each grouping resembles a little umbrella or sunshade, hence the name. To keep within bounds cut the main trunk and let it remain a pot-bound cluster plant.

LOCATION: Thrives in average house temperature and dry air. Ideal for apartment dwellers. Give filtered sun, but good light. East or west window.

HEIGHT: Tall—to 6 feet or more, but more appealing if kept a lot smaller.

WATERING: Soak, permit to dry completely, then rewater.

PROPAGATION: Pot individually the suckers that cluster around the main stem.

◀ VENUS FLYTRAP (*Dionaea muscipula*)

A weird botanical item that sets a trap for its victims. Each half of the trap has three trigger hairs. If an insect touches any one of these, the trap snaps shut. Within are fluids to digest the hapless creature. This insectivorous plant, native to the savannas of South Carolina, does especially well under glass. A bell jar or terrarium successfully simulates the moisture-laden air of its native habitat. If you have no flies about, touch the leaves with a pencil occasionally just to watch them spring shut. After a few minutes they open again. With no insects to dine upon, the Venus flytrap derives its nourishment from the soil.

LOCATION: Full sun. Temperature preferred 60° F.

HEIGHT: Low—to 6 inches.

SOIL: Grows in sphagnum moss with a little sand and rich leaf mold added.

WATERING: Keep moist all the time. Spray tops frequently.

103

◄ VERBENA (*Verbena* 'Chiquita')

An extremely decorative everblooming pot plant with vivid scarlet flower heads in great profusion. The innumerable stems curve and trail forming a curtain of green, starred with red flowers. The foliage is soft and feathery and in shape and form resembles the fronds of a fern.

LOCATION: Full sun, south window.

HEIGHT: Climbs and trails.

SOIL: Ordinary garden loam with compost added.

WATERING. Average

PROPAGATION: When mature the plant separates readily at the roots.

## VOODOO PLANT, LIZARD ARUM (*Sauromatum guttatum*)

This mysterious bulb grows and flowers with neither soil nor water, and not even a pot! Merely set it on a shelf somewhere and watch what happens. From the bulb emerges an exotic calla lily-like spathe with bright red polka dots. This surrounds the tonguelike spadix, which is a cluster of miniature flowers. If you put it in the garden for the summer, or in a container of earth after the bloom passes, another surprise is in store. Weird yellow and ◄ purple-brown leaves, slim and tapering, develop.

LOCATION: Filtered sun, set on mantel, desk, or table. Light essential and some sun preferred.

HEIGHT: Low—to 10 inches.

SOIL: None needed until after flowering. Then pot in rich loam, or if the weather is warm enough, sink the bulb loose in the garden until fall. At that time, dry off again, and allow to remain dry, stored perhaps on a closet shelf, for several weeks. Then bring to its usual position for another blooming season.

WATERING: After it has finished flowering and is potted, water, let dry, then rewater.

WANDERING JEW (*Zebrina pendula*)

A native of tropical Mexico and Central America and a member of a large family, many with colorful leaves and many that climb and trail. The assorted varieties have different textures and markings. Each leaf of this particular one is a three-toned color scheme; the underside is maroon, the surface dark green and the veins pale green. The foliage tints deepen in full sun and are lighter in shade.

LOCATION: Thrives in semi-shade, but with less colorful leaves. Full sun or partial sun preferred.

HEIGHT: Climbs and trails. ►

SOIL: Will grow for long periods in water. But eventually needs average garden loam.

WATERING: Should be watered generously, the roots kept moist most of the time.

PROPAGATION: Four-inch branch tips will root in water, or when the bottom inch or two is buried in a pot of soil.

SPECIAL CARE: To keep full and compact some of the runners can be led back and anchored in the plant center.

WALKING ANTHERICUM, SPIDER ▶
PLANT (*Chlorophytum elatum vittatum*)

A South African plant that thrives in a
warm dry atmosphere. Streamers of green
leaves, each with a white stripe down the
middle, arch out of the center like a
fountain. New plantlets, miniature editions
of the parent, appear at the end of runners.
Small flowers open on the runners just
before the new plantlets form.

LOCATION: Filtered sun, full sun. South,
east or west window. Grow on a shelf, or
in a hanging basket, so that the streamers
of offspring can trail over the edges.

HEIGHT: Medium. Give ample space
horizontally.

SOIL: Ordinary garden loam with compost added.

WATERING: More than average. Water;
when nearly dry, water again.

PROPAGATION: When small plantlets
have six or seven leaves, pot them separately, or root these in water and then pot.
Even simpler, pin a plantlet down in a
neighboring pot while still attached to its
parent. When new growth commences, cut
it apart.

◀ WANDERING JEW (*Cyanotis
veldthoutiana*)

A new plant, sometimes sold under the
name of Tradescantia 'White Gossamer.'
Its leaves mature to fresh soft pink. The
foliage is covered with velvety gossamer.
Three-petaled lavender blooms with golden
stamens appear here and there among the
soft downy leaves.

LOCATION: Full sun, filtered sun, and it
even tolerates shade. But leaf colors deepen
in full sun, and pale in shade.

HEIGHT: Climbs and trails. Needs ample
space horizontally.

SOIL: Ordinary garden loam. Will also
grow in water.

WATERING: Average. Soil should be
allowed to dry between soakings.

PROPAGATION: At any time of year four-
to six-inch cuttings may be set with the
bottom end of each an inch or two under
the soil. In a few weeks these root. They
will also root in a jar of water.

SPECIAL CARE: To keep the plant compact, and from becoming stringy, a branch
or two can be bent back and pinned down
in the center of the pot with a hairpin.

WAX PLANT (*Hoya carnosa variegata*)

Named for Thomas Hoy, the eighteenth-century gardener of the Duke of Northumberland. This enthusiastic man of the soil always watered and tended the wax plants before any others in the duke's palatial greenhouses, and was usually to be found somewhere near his favorites. Leathery, oval leaves of this variety have white rims that mature to pink; the pink-tinted flowers age white. In late winter, the creamy porcelain-like blossoms with chocolate centers form in prim clusters and emit an exotic perfume.

LOCATION: South, east, or west window. Good light is vital.

HEIGHT: Climbs and trails. Give a piece of bark or small trellis in the pot to climb on.

SOIL: Compost, leaf mold, and sand. For prolific flowering grow pot-bound.

WATERING: Keep dry in autumn, and water copiously in late winter when in bud and flower.

PROPAGATION: Aerial roots along the stem reach out from a mature plant. If these are given earth to grow in, they soon become new plants.

SPECIAL CARE: In autumn keep cool and dry with only enough water to prevent the leaves from shriveling, but give weekly plant food. In January bring to warmth, increase the water supply and spray foliage. Handle carefully, leaving the new spurs undisturbed, as they are the source of flowers and next year's blooms will also be on them.

WINGED PEA (*Lotus berthelotii*) ▶

Festoons of dense, silvery, fernlike foliage trail and spill from a hanging basket or a pot on the window-garden shelf. Red flowers with long twisted parting petals hang down all through the soft foliage

LOCATION: Full sun. Does best in a south window.

HEIGHT: Climbs, spreads, and trails. Needs ample room.

SOIL: Ordinary garden loam.

WATERING: Less than average. Soil should remain dry several days between waterings.

WEEPING LAUREL (*Ficus benjamina*)
From India. Like other members of the
*Ficus* family, this large decorative house
plant is sturdy and tolerates a certain
amount of shade. The graceful branches,
with their small, shiny, oval leaves slightly
pointed at the tips, form a real tree. If you
have plenty of space, you will enjoy having
the fun of growing a regular tree indoors
in winter—and the year round.

LOCATION: Full sun, no sun, or anywhere
in between.

HEIGHT: Tall—to 8 feet. Plenty of space
needed.

SOIL: Ordinary garden loam.

WATERING: Average. Water, let dry,
and then rewater.

107

# Seven Window Gardens

A little plotting, planning and choosing is the key to a successful indoor garden of innumerable exciting and lovely plants. Select the plants that are right for you and your surroundings. Here are seven quite different indoor-garden plans to help you start. All the plants are included in the preceding section.

Suppose you have a north window, light aplenty, but no sun; there is a special garden for you. If you have a favorite collection of vases, you can use them all to grow a window garden with every plant in water instead of soil. Perhaps you would like a window in which either the flowers or the foliage of every plant has a fragrance. Or have you never grown a plant indoors before? There is a beginners' group for you that will thrive willy-nilly. A garden of gay and giddy foliage plants also awaits. Or would a garden of cool, quiet greens be just the thing? Perhaps best of all, if you have plenty of sun, would be a rainbow of continuous blooms from October to May. Each plant in this garden flowers two months or more without ceasing!

Also, of course, you can be independent, and run through all the possibilities, pick and choose this and that, and compose your own window garden. However you do it, whatever plants you select, it is a new world you are entering, and a thrilling one.

· 1 ·

## GARDEN FOR CONTINUOUS BLOOM AND COLOR

This window garden, a riot of brilliant colors, thrives in a southern exposure. Here tall, dignified callas, dancing lantanas, and neat primroses blend their tones to bring you the atmosphere and gay tints of summertime. Between fall and spring, each plant included blooms for at least two months and often longer. Primroses, shrimp plant, lantana, browallia and sometimes the crown of thorns will begin flowering in the autumn and never stop until spring. (Fourteen plants, seven different varieties.)

1. *Lantana*
2. *Shrimp Plant*
3. *Primrose*
4. *Browallia*
5. *Crown of Thorns*
6. *Christmas Cactus*
7. *Calla Lily*

# Garden for Fragrance

A window garden of plants to be grown for fragrance either of foliage or of flowers. These all thrive in sun or part sun. Every plant brings a sweet scent either in its flower or leaf. The scents are most pungent in the morning sunlight and after watering, when they merge and mingle into a true symphony of fragrances. (Fourteen different plants, fourteen different varieties.)

1. *Orchid Cactus*
2. *Wax Plant*
3. *Sweet Olive*
4. *Lemon Vine Cactus*
5. *Bouvardia*
6. *Peppermint Geranium*
7. *Nutmeg Geranium*
8. *Honey Bells*
9. *Clerodendrum*
10. *Gardenia*
11. *Peruvian Daffodil*
12. *Amazon Lily*
13. *Rose Geranium*
14. *Persian Lime*

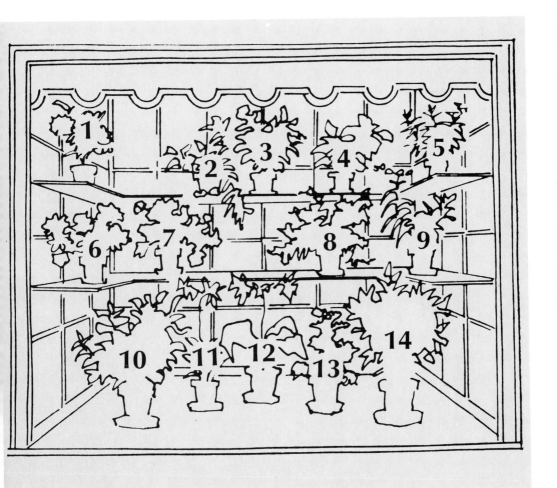

## · 3 ·

## GARDEN FOR BEGINNERS

Suppose you have never grown a house plant before but yearn to try your hand at window gardening. Here is a foolproof group of plants that are tough and hardy. All flourish in full sun and bring you fragrance, color and contrasting textures. The sea onion is one of the easiest and best of all. Each year it sheds its skin to reveal beneath a cluster of bulblets. Pot them for a new group of plants. (Thirteen plants, thirteen different varieties.)

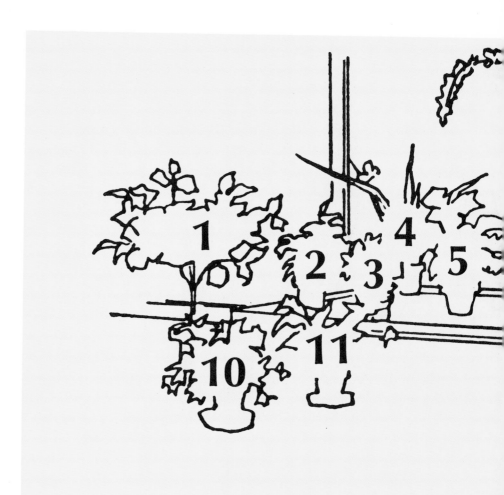

1. *Lemon Tree*
2. *Patience*
3. *Grape Ivy*
4. *Fan Iris*
5. *Common Red Geranium*
6. *Begonia ('Fiesta')*
7. *Sea Onion*
8. *Crown of Thorns*
9. *Jerusalem Cherry*
10. *Philodendron*
11. *Begonia ('Iron Cross')*
12. *Marguerite*
13. *Snailflower*

## · 4 ·

## GARDEN GROWN IN WATER

Here is a window garden in which all the plants will thrive for a season in water. Take this opportunity to use attractive glass vases. Use some very clear glass containers, if possible, and have the fun of watching the continual development of roots. For best results grow these plants in filtered sunlight. (Thirteen plants, eight different varieties.)

1. *Chinese Evergreen*
2. *Corn Plant*
3. *Coleus*
4. *Philodendron (common)*
5. *Glacier Ivy*
6. *Bloodleaf*
7. *Wandering Jew*
8. *Umbrella Sedge*

## · 5 ·

## GARDEN FOR NORTH WINDOW

Even without sun at all, if you have good light in your window an indoor garden not only of greenery but with some flowers will flourish. All these plants will also do well in an east or west exposure. African violets in four different colors thrive and bloom abundantly in a window with good light and with little or no sun. Here is a pleasing assortment of greenery to go with them, and each plant in the group has some particular merit. For instance, when you grow a piggyback you will have the fun of watching new plantlets form on top of parent leaves. (Fourteen plants, ten different varieties.)

1. *Kangaroo Vine*
2. *String-of-Hearts*
3. *African Violet (pink)*
4. *African Violet (blue)*
5. *African Violet (lavender)*
6. *African Violet (white)*
7. *Feather Ivy*
8. *Philodendron (common)*
9. *Caladium*
10. *Glacier Ivy*
11. *Ivy ('Meagheri')*
12. *Windowleaf Philodendron*
13. *Piggyback Plant*

## · 6 ·

# GARDEN OF GAY, VIVID FOLIAGE PLANTS

This garden of variegated foliage plants thrives in sun or part sun. Gay, tinted leaves and patterned foliage contribute as much color to the indoor garden as blossoms would. In full sun the leaf rim of both the sunset geranium and aurora borealis turns vivid pink. Blood-leaf foliage is translucent, and when the sun shines through it, the whole room appears to be pink-tinted. (Thirteen plants, thirteen different varieties.)

1. *Anthurium*
2. *Aurora Borealis*
3. *Geranium ('Sunset')*
4. *String-of-Hearts*
5. *Geranium ('Skies of Italy')*
6. *Strawberry Geranium*
7. *Croton*
8. *Wandering Jew*
9. *Caladium*
10. *Velvet Plant*
11. *Coleus ('Ruffle Beauty')*
12. *Bloodleaf*
13. *Rabbit's-foot Fern*

## · 7 ·

## GARDEN OF COOL, QUIET GREENS

These green-foliage plants in a variety of shades will thrive in an east or west window, or with filtered sunlight. For you who like to feel as well as look at plants, each one has a contrasting texture. How firm and smooth is the bird's-nest fern to touch, how delicate the Maidenhair. Run your hand along the symmetrical branches of the Norfolk Island pine, and gently touch the baby's tears. (Fourteen different plants, fourteen different varieties.)

1. *Kangaroo Vine*
2. *Holly Fern*
3. *Creeping Fig*
4. *Geranium ('French Lace')*
5. *Baby's Tears*
6. *Bird's-nest Fern*
7. *Ivy 'Pittsburgh'*
8. *Rose Geranium*
9. *Norfolk Island Pine*
10. *Grape Ivy*
11. *Peppermint Geranium*
12. *Maidenhair Fern*
13. *Feather Ivy*
14. *Rabbit's-foot Fern*

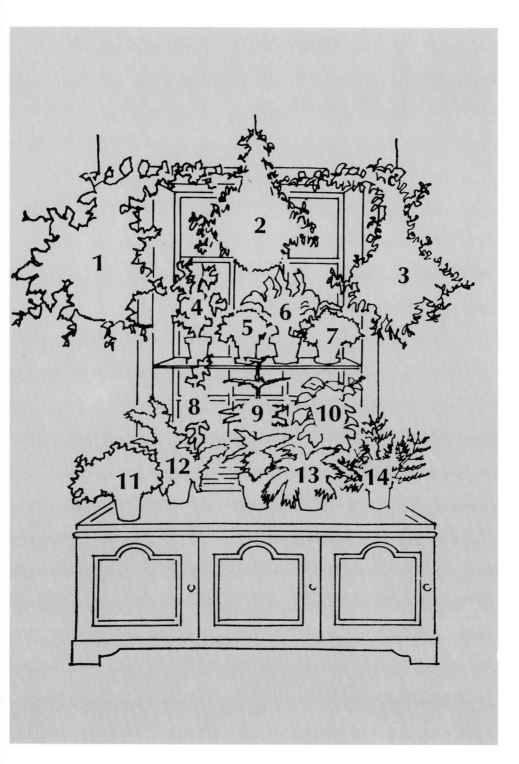

# Index

Abutilon hybridium, 63
Acalypha
  hispida, 47
  wilkesiana, 49
Adiantum tenerum 'Wrightii,' 57
Aechmea 'Foster's Favorite,' 78
African violet, 13, 18, 27
Aglaeonema
  commutatum, 47
  treubii, 47
Aloe
  arborescens, 28
  candelabra, 28
  vera, 39
Amaryllis, 29
Amazon lily, 28, 111
American Wonder Lemon, 9, 76, 113
Anthurium
  andraeanum, 29
  crystallinum, 30
  scherzerianum, 30
Aphids, 13–14
Aporocactus flagelliformis, 44
Araucaria excelsa, 80
Artillery plant, 30
Asparagus fern, 31
Asparagus sprengeri, 31
Asplenium
  bulbiferum, 58
  nidus, 55
Astrophytum
  asterias, 44
  myriostigma, 41
Aurora borealis, 9, 31, 118
Australian flame pea, 32
Australian silk oak, 96

Australian umbrella tree, 103
Azalea, 33
Aztec lily, 32

Baby tears, 32, 120
Banana, ladyfinger, 75
Barbados gooseberry, 40
Begonia, 19–20, 33–35, 99
  corallina de Lucerna, 34
  dancing girl, 34
  eyelash, 34
  fern, 35
  fiesta, 35, 112
  Iron Cross, 35, 113
  Merry Christmas, 35
  strawberry, 99
  watermelon, 87
Begonia
  boweri, 34
  haageana, 33
  semperflorens, 35
Beloperone guttata, 95
Billbergia 'fantasia,' 36
Bird of Paradise, 36
Bloodleaf, 37, 115, 119
Bougainvillea, 37
Bouvardia, 'Fire Chief,' 37, 110
Bouvardia ternifolia, 37, 110
Boxwood, 38
Brassavola nodosa, 83
Brazilian edelweiss, 38
Brazilian firecracker, 38
Brilliant star, 74
Browallia speciosa major, 39, 108
Burn plant, 39
Burro's tail, 39
Buxus microphylla japonica, 38

Cactus, 40–44
  Barbados gooseberry, 40
  Bishop's cap, 41
  *Cerius monstrosus,* 40
  Christmas, 42
  Lemon vine, 40, 111
  Notocactus, 42
  Old man, 43
  Orchid, 43, 111
  Rat-tail, 44
  Sand-dollar, 44
Caladium, 45, 117, 118
*Camellia japonica,* 46
*Campanula isophylla,* 99
Cape primrose, 100
Carrot fern, 21
Cattleya varieties, *see* Orchid
*Cephalocereus senilis,* 43
*Cereus*
  *monstrosus,* 40
  *peruvianus,* 40
*Ceropegia*
  night-blooming, 9
  *sandersonii,* 46
  *woodii,* 100
*Certomium falcatum* 'Rocheford-
  *ianium compactum,'* 57
*Cestrum parqui,* 72
Chameleon, 15
Chenille plant, 47
Cherry, Christmas, 73, 113
Cherry, Jerusalem, 73, 113
Chinese bellflower, 63
Chinese evergreen, 47, 115
Chinese holly, 54
*Chlorophytum elatum vittatum,*
  105
*Chorizema cordatum,* 32
Christmas cherry, 73, 113
Christ's thorn, 50
*Cissus*
  *antarctica,* 75
  *rhombifolia,* 69
*Citrus*
  *aurantifolia,* 78
  *limonia* 'Ponderosa,' 76
  *taitensis,* 81
*Clerodendrum thomsoniae,* 48
*Clivia miniata,* 77

*Coccoloba uvifera,* 93
*Codiaeum,* 51
Coleus, 48, 115
  'Ruffle Beauty,' 48, 118
*Columnea microphylla,* 49
Copperleaf, 49
Corkscrew flower, 96
Corn plant, 49, 114
*Costus igneus,* 98
*Crassula arborescens,* 72
*Crinum bulbisperum,* 51
Crinum lily, 51
*Crossandra infundibuliformis,* 50
Croton, 51, 119
Crown of thorns, 3, 50, 108, 112
*Cyanotis veldthoutiana,* 105
*Cyclamen persicum,* 51
*Cyperus alternifolius,* 102
*Cyrtomium falcatum* 'Rochefordia-
  *num compactum,'* 57

Daffodil, Peruvian, 87, 111
*Darlingtonia californica,* 52
*Davallia canariensis,* 58
Devil's ivy, 52
*Dieffenbachia maculata,* 53
*Dionaea muscipula,* 103
*Dizygotheca elegantissima,* 62
*Dracaena fragrans massangeana,* 49
Dumb cane, 53

*Echeveria glauca,* 53
Edelweiss, Brazilian, 38
eggshell pots, 23
Emerald feather, 31
*Epidendrum radicans,* 82
*Epiphyllum*
  hybrids, 43
*Eucharis grandiflora,* 28
*Euonymous japonica microphyllus,*
  52
*Euphorbia*
  *lactea,* 54
  *milii,* 50
  *pulcherrima,* 90

False holly, 54
Fan iris, 55
Fan palms, 76

124

Fancy-leaved caladium, 45
Felicia amelloides, 79
Fern, 13, 55–59
    Asparagus, 31
    Bird's-nest, 55, 118, 119
    Boston, 56
    False hare's foot, 56
    Holly, 57, 121
    Lace, 57
    Maidenhair, 57, 121
    Mother, 58
    Rabbit's-foot, 58, 119, 121
    Silver-lace, 58
    Staghorn, 59
    Victoria bracken, 59
Ficus
    benjamina, 107
    diversifolia, 61
    elastica, 92
    lyrata, 60
    pumila, 61
    radicans variegata, 60
Fig
    creeping, 61, 121
    fiddle-leaf, 60
    mistletoe, 61
Finger aralia, 62
Fingernail plant, 62
Firedragon, 49
Fittonia argyroneura, 80
Flamingo flower, 63
Flies, 4
Flowering maple, 63
Food, plant, 13
Friendship plant, 72
Fuchsia, 14
    magellanica gracilis, 64

Gardenia jasminoides, 64, 110
Geogenanthus undatus, 94
Geranium, 13, 65–68
    apple, 9, 65
    cinnamon, 65
    common red varieties, 65, 112
    'Dr. Livingston,' 66
    'French Lace,' 66, 121
    ivy ('L'élégant'), 67
    ivy (peltatum 'Willy'), 66
    ivy ('Sunset'), 67, 119

Geranium, continued
    miniature (hortorum 'Pigmy'),
        67
    nutmeg, 9, 65, 111
    peppermint, 67, 111, 121
    rose, 9, 10, 68, 111, 120
    'Skies of Italy,' 68, 118
    strawberry, 99, 119
German ivy, 69
Gloxinia, 13, 69
Grape ivy, 69, 112, 120
Grevillea robusta, 96
Gynura aurantiaca, 102

Hedera
    helix 'Glacier,' 71
    helix 'Pittsburgh,' 71
    Meagheri, 71
Helxine soleirolii, 32
Hibiscus rosa-sinensis, 70
Hippeastrum, 29
Holly fern, 57, 121
Honey bells, 68, 110
Howeia forsteriana, 76
Hoya carnosa variegata, 106
Hymenocallis calathina, 87

Impatiens sultanii, 86
Inch plant, 70
Insecticide, use of, 13–15
Iresine herbstii, 37
Iris, 11, 55, 113
Irish moss, 32
Italian bellflower, 99
Ivy, 13, 14, 19, 69, 71
    devil's, 52
    feather, 71, 117, 120
    geranium, 66, 67
    German, 69
    Glacier, 71, 114, 116
    grape, 69, 112, 120
    parlor, 69
    'Pittsburgh,' 71, 121
    water, 69

Jacobinia suberecta, 63
Jade plant, 72
Japanese laurel, 72
Japanese rubber plant, 72

Jasmine, 74
Jerusalem cherry, 73, 113
Jessamine, 72

Kalanchoe
  blossfeldiana, 74
  daigremontiana, 74
  fedtschenkoi marginata, 31
  tomentosa, 86
Kangaroo vine, 75
Kentia palm, 76

Ladyfinger banana, 75
Lady of the Night (Orchid), 83
Lady's-eardrops, 64
Lantana, 14, 109
  montevidensis, 77
Laurel
  Japanese, 72
  weeping, 107
Lemon, American Wonder, 76, 113
Lemon vine, 40
Leopard plant, 76
Ligularia Kaempferi 'Aureo-macu-
  lata,' 76
Lily
  Calla, 45, 109
  Crinum, 51
  Kaffir, 77
Lily-of-the-valley orchid, 83
Lime, Persian, 78, 110
Lithops, 99
Living vase, 27, 78
Lizard arum, 104
Lotus berthelotii, 106

Mahernia verticillata, 68
Manettia bicolor, 38
Maple, flowering, 63
Maranta leuconeura 'Kerchoveana,'
  91
Marguerite, blue, 79, 113
Mealy bugs, 14
Mimosa pudica, 95
Monstera deliciosa, 88
Moses-in-a-boat, 79
Moses-in-the-cradle, 79
Moses-on-a-raft, 79
Mother-in-law plant, 53

Mother-of-thousands, 89
Musa cavendishii, 75
Myrtle, 78
Myrtus communis microphylla, 78

Neomarica northiana, 55
Neoregelia spectabilis, 62
Nephrolepsis exaltata
  'Bostoniensis,' 56
  'Whitmanii,' 57
Nerium oleander, 81
Nerve plant, 80
Nicotiana, 14
Norfolk Island pine, 80, 121
Notocactus leninghausii, 42
Nursery, 18

Oak
  Australian silk, 96
  flowering, 32
Odontoglossum pulchelium, 83
Oleander, 81
Olive, sweet, 11, 101, 111
Oncidium triquetrum, 82
Orange, 81
Orchid, 13, 81, 82–83
  cattleya varieties, 81
  epidendrum radicans, 82
  lady of the night, 83
  lily-of-the-valley, 83
  oncidium triquetrum, 82
  paphiopedilum 'Olivia,' 82
Ornithogalum caudatum, 94
Osmanthus
  fragrans, 101
  ilicifolius variegatus, 54
Otaheite, 81
Oxalis, 84–85
  martiana 'Aurea-reticulata,' 84
  ortgiesii, 84
  variabilis, 84–85

Painted nettle, 48
Palm
  Fan, 76
  Kentia, 76
  Paradise, 76
  Pigmy date, 85
Panda plant, 86

Paphiopedilum 'Olivia,' 82
Paradise palm, 76
Parlor ivy, 69
Patience, 86, 112, 113
Patient Lucy, 86
Pebble plant, 99
Pebble tray, 1
Pelargonium, see Geranium
Peperomia Sanderii argyreia, 87
Pereskia aculeata, 40
Persian lime, 78, 110
Peruvian daffodil, 87, 110
Pests, 13–15
Phaseolus caracalla, 97
Philodendron, 13, 19, 87, 88, 113,
    114, 115, 116
    Monstera deliciosa, 88
    Oxycardium, 88
    Windowleaf, 88, 116
    x Mandianum, 87
Phoenix roebelenii, 85
Piggyback plant, 89, 117
Pilea
    involucrata, 89
    microphylla, 30
Pine, Norfolk Island, 80, 121
Pineapple rosette, 22
Pineapple sage, 89
Pitcher plant, 91
Plans for window gardens, 108–121
Platycerium bifurcatum 'bloomii,'
    59
Poinsettia, 90
Polypodium aureum 'Mandaianum,'
    56
Potato vine, 21
Prayer plant, 9, 91
Primrose, 90, 108, 109
    Cape, 100
Primula malacoides, 90
Pteris
    argyraea, 58
    ensiformis 'Victoriae,' 59
Pyrethrum, 14

Rechsteineria leucotricha, 38
Red-hot cattail, 47
Repotting, 15–17
Resurrection plant, 91

Rhododendron 'Albert and Eliza-
    beth,' 33
Rhoeo spathacea, 79
Rosa chinensis minima, 92
Rosa rouletti, 92
Rose, miniature, 92
Rosmarinus officinalis, 93
Rosemary, 93
Rotenone, 14
Rubber plant, 92
    Japanese, 72
Ruffle Beauty' coleus, 48, 118

Saintpaulia ionanthe, 27
Salvia rutilans, 89
Sansevieria trifasciata, 97
Sarracenia purpurea, 91
Sauromatum guttatum, 104
Saxifraga
    sarmentosa, 99
Scale, 14
Scarlet gnome, 74
Schefflera actinophylla, 103
Schlumbergera bridgesii, 42
Scindapsus 'Wilcox,' 52
Sea grape, 93
Sea onion, 94, 112
Sedum morganianum, 39
Seersucker plant, 9, 94
Selaginella lepidophylla, 91
Senecio mikanioides, 69
Sensitive plant, 95
Shower of gold, 50
Shrimp plant, 95, 109
Siderasis fuscata, 13, 96
Sinningia speciosa, 69
Smithiantha zebrina, 101
Snailflower, 97, 113
Snake plant, 97
Solanum pseudo-capsicum, 73
Spathe flower, 98
Spathiphyllum cannaefolium, 98
Spider plant, 105
Spiders, red, 14
Spiral flag, 98
Spiral ginger, 98
Stapelia gigantea, 32
Star-of-Bethlehem, 99
Stone-and-window plant, 99

Strawberry begonia, 99
Strawberry geranium, 99
*Strelitzia reginae,* 36
*Streptocarpus saxorum,* 100
String-of-hearts vine, 100, 116, 119
Summering, 17
Sweet olive, 11, 101, 111

Temple bells, 101
*Tillandsia cyanea,* 101
*Tolmiea menziesii,* 89
*Trachelospermum jasminoides,* 74
*Tradescantia*
    *albiflora 'Albovittata,'* 70
    'White Gossamer,' 105

Umbrella sedge, 12, 102, 114
Umbrella tree, Australian, 103

Velvet plant, 102, 118

Venus fly trap, 9, 103
Verbena, 'Chiquita,' 104
Vine
    Kangaroo, 75, 116, 120
    Passion, 9
    Rosary, 100
    String-of-hearts, 100, 116, 119
Voodoo plant, 104

Walking anthericum, 105
Wandering Jew, 104, 105, 115, 118
Watering, 12–13, 20
Water ivy, 69
Watermelon begonia, 87
Wax plant, 106, 111
Weeping laurel, 107
Winged pea, 106

*Zantedeschia aethiopica,* 45
*Zebrina pendula,* 105